Apollo to the Moon

General Editor

William H. Goetzmann
Jack S. Blanton, Sr., Chair in History
  University of Texas at Austin

Consulting Editor

Tom D. Crouch
Chairman, Department of Aeronautics
  National Air and Space Museum
  Smithsonian Institution

WORLD EXPLORERS

Apollo to the Moon

Gregory P. Kennedy

Introductory Essay by Michael Collins

CHELSEA HOUSE PUBLISHERS

New York · Philadelphia

On the cover The moon, featuring the Sea of Tranquility; astronaut Buzz Aldrin on the lunar surface.

Chelsea House Publishers
Editor-in-Chief Remmel Nunn
Managing Editor Karyn Gullen Browne
Copy Chief Mark Rifkin
Picture Editor Adrian G. Allen
Art Director Maria Epes
Assistant Art Director Noreen Romano
Series Design Loraine Machlin
Manufacturing Director Gerald Levine
Systems Manager Lindsey Ottman
Production Manager Joseph Romano
Production Coordinator Marie Claire Cebrián

World Explorers
Senior Editor Sean Dolan

Staff for APOLLO TO THE MOON
Associate Editor Terrance Dolan
Copy Editor Christopher Duffy
Assistant Editor Martin Mooney
Picture Researcher Alan Gottlieb
Senior Designer Basia Niemczyc

5 7 9 8 6

Library of Congress Cataloging-in-Publication Data

Kennedy, Gregory P.
  Apollo to the moon/Gregory P. Kennedy
    p. cm.—(World explorers)
  Includes bibliographical references and index.
  Summary: A summary of NASA's Apollo project that put the first man on the moon.
  ISBN 0-7910-1322-7
       0-7910-1546-7 (pbk.)
  1. Project Apollo (U.S.)—Juvenile literature. [1. Project Apollo (U.S.) 2. Space flight to the moon.] I. Title. II. Series.
                                          91-22591
TL799.M6K45 1992   CIP
629.45′4—dc20   AC

CONTENTS

WORLD EXPLORERS

THE EARLY EXPLORERS

Herodotus and the Explorers of the Classical Age
Marco Polo and the Medieval Explorers
The Viking Explorers

THE FIRST GREAT AGE OF DISCOVERY

Jacques Cartier, Samuel de Champlain, and the Explorers of Canada
Christopher Columbus and the First Voyages to the New World
From Coronado to Escalante: The Explorers of the Spanish Southwest
Hernando de Soto and the Explorers of the American South
Sir Francis Drake and the Struggle for an Ocean Empire
Vasco da Gama and the Portuguese Explorers
La Salle and the Explorers of the Mississippi
Ferdinand Magellan and the Discovery of the World Ocean
Pizarro, Orellana, and the Exploration of the Amazon
The Search for the Northwest Passage
Giovanni da Verrazano and the Explorers of the Atlantic Coast

THE SECOND GREAT AGE OF DISCOVERY

Roald Amundsen and the Quest for the South Pole
Daniel Boone and the Opening of the Ohio Country
Captain James Cook and the Explorers of the Pacific
The Explorers of Alaska
John Charles Frémont and the Great Western Reconnaissance
Alexander von Humboldt, Colossus of Exploration
Lewis and Clark and the Route to the Pacific
Alexander Mackenzie and the Explorers of Canada
Robert Peary and the Quest for the North Pole
Zebulon Pike and the Explorers of the American Southwest
John Wesley Powell and the Great Surveys of the American West
Jedediah Smith and the Mountain Men of the American West
Henry Stanley and the European Explorers of Africa
Lt. Charles Wilkes and the Great U.S. Exploring Expedition

THE THIRD GREAT AGE OF DISCOVERY

Apollo to the Moon
The Explorers of the Undersea World
The First Men in Space
The Mission to Mars and Beyond
Probing Deep Space

CHELSEA HOUSE PUBLISHERS

Into the Unknown

Michael Collins

It is difficult to define most eras in history with any precision, but not so the space age. On October 4, 1957, it burst on us with little warning when the Soviet Union launched *Sputnik*, a 184-pound cannonball that circled the globe once every 96 minutes. Less than 4 years later, the Soviets followed this first primitive satellite with the flight of Yury Gagarin, a 27-year-old fighter pilot who became the first human to orbit the earth. The Soviet Union's success prompted President John F. Kennedy to decide that the United States should "land a man on the moon and return him safely to earth" before the end of the 1960s. We now had not only a space age but a space race.

I was born in 1930, exactly the right time to allow me to participate in Project Apollo, as the U.S. lunar program came to be known. As a young man growing up, I often found myself too young to do the things I wanted—or suddenly too old, as if someone had turned a switch at midnight. But for Apollo, 1930 was the perfect year to be born, and I was very lucky. In 1966 I enjoyed circling the earth for three days, and in 1969 I flew to the moon and laughed at the sight of the tiny earth, which I could cover with my thumbnail.

How the early explorers would have loved the view from space! With one glance Christopher Columbus could have plotted his course and reassured his crew that the world was indeed round. In 90 minutes Magellan could have looked down at every port of call in the *Victoria's* three-year circumnavigation of the globe. Given a chance to map their route from orbit, Lewis and Clark could have told President Jefferson that there was no easy Northwest Passage but that a continent of exquisite diversity awaited their scrutiny.

In a physical sense, we have already gone to most places that we can. That is not to say that there are not new adventures awaiting us deep in the sea or on the red plains of Mars, but more important than reaching new places will be understanding those we have already visited. There are vital gaps in our understanding of how our planet works as an ecosystem and how our planet fits into the infinite order of the universe. The next great age may well be the age of assimilation, in which we use microscope and telescope to evaluate what we have discovered and put that knowledge to use. The adventure of being first to reach may be replaced by the satisfaction of being first to grasp. Surely that is a form of exploration as vital to our well-being, and perhaps even survival, as the distinction of being the first to explore a specific geographical area.

The explorers whose stories are told in the books of this series did not just sail perilous seas, scale rugged mountains, traverse blistering deserts, dive to the depths of the ocean, or land on the moon. Their voyages and expeditions were journeys of mind as much as of time and distance, through which they—and all of mankind—were able to reach a greater understanding of our universe. That challenge remains, for all of us. The imperative is to see, to understand, to develop knowledge that others can use, to help nurture this planet that sustains us all. Perhaps being born in 1975 will be as lucky for a new generation of explorer as being born in 1930 was for Neil Armstrong, Buzz Aldrin, and Mike Collins.

The Reader's Journey

William H. Goetzmann

This volume is one of a series that takes us with the great explorers of the ages on bold journeys over the oceans and the continents and into outer space. As we travel along with these imaginative and courageous journeyers, we share their adventures and their knowledge. We also get a glimpse of that mysterious and inextinguishable fire that burned in the breast of men such as Magellan and Columbus—the fire that has propelled all those throughout the ages who have been driven to leave behind family and friends for a voyage into the unknown.

No one has ever satisfactorily explained the urge to explore, the drive to go to the "back of beyond." It is certain that it has been present in man almost since he began walking erect and first ventured across the African savannas. Sparks from that same fire fueled the transoceanic explorers of the Ice Age, who led their people across the vast plain that formed a land bridge between Asia and North America, and the astronauts and scientists who determined that man must reach the moon.

Besides an element of adventure, all exploration involves an element of mystery. We must not confuse exploration with discovery. Exploration is a purposeful human activity—a search for something. Discovery may be the end result of that search; it may also be an accident, as when Columbus found a whole new world while searching for the Indies. Often, the explorer may not even realize the full significance of what he has discovered, as was the case with Columbus. Exploration, on the other hand, is the product of a cultural or individual curiosity; it is a unique process that has enabled mankind to know and understand the world's oceans, continents, and polar regions. It is at the heart of scientific thinking. One of its most significant aspects is that it teaches people to ask the right questions; by doing so, it forces us to reevaluate what we think we know and understand. Thus knowledge progresses, and we are driven constantly to a new awareness and appreciation of the universe in all its infinite variety.

The motivation for exploration is not always pure. In his fascination with the new, man often forgets that others have been there before him. For example, the popular notion of the discovery of America overlooks the complex Indian civilizations that had existed there for thousands of years before the arrival of Europeans. Man's desire for conquest, riches, and fame is often linked inextricably with his quest for the unknown, but a story that touches so closely on the human essence must of necessity treat war as well as peace, avarice with generosity, both pride and humility, frailty and greatness. The story of exploration is above all a story of humanity and of man's understanding of his place in the universe.

The WORLD EXPLORERS series has been divided into four sections. The first treats the explorers of the ancient world, the Viking explorers of the 9th through the 11th centuries, and Marco Polo and the medieval explorers. The rest of the series is divided into three great ages of exploration. The first is the era of Columbus and Magellan: the period spanning the 15th and 16th centuries, which saw the discovery and exploration of the New World and the world ocean. The second might be called the age of science and imperialism, the era made possible by the scientific advances of the 17th century, which witnessed the discovery of the world's last two undiscovered continents, Australia and Antarctica, the mapping of all the continents and oceans, and the establishment of colonies all over the world. The third great age refers to the most ambitious quests of the 20th century—the probing of space and of the ocean's depths.

As we reach out into the darkness of outer space and other galaxies, we come to better understand how our ancestors confronted *oecumene,* or the vast earthly unknown. We learn once again the meaning of an unknown 18th-century sea captain's advice to navigators:

> And if by chance you make a landfall on the shores of another sea in a far country inhabited by savages and barbarians, remember you this: the greatest danger and the surest hope lies not with fires and arrows but in the quicksilver hearts of men.

At its core, exploration is a series of moral dramas. But it is these dramas, involving new lands, new people, and exotic ecosystems of staggering beauty, that make the explorers' stories not only moral tales but also some of the greatest adventure stories ever recorded. They represent the process of learning in its most expansive and vivid forms. We see that real life, past and present, transcends even the adventures of the starship *Enterprise.*

"We've Got a Bad Fire"

Apollo 1 *insignia*

At about one o'clock on the afternoon of January 27, 1967, the prime crew for NASA's first manned Apollo flight arrived at launchpad complex 34, Cape Canaveral, Florida. Astronauts Virgil I. ("Gus") Grissom, Edward H. White, and Roger Chaffee, moving slowly in their cumbersome pressure suits, rode the elevator to the top of the service-umbilical tower, crossed through the control room, and settled into the cabin of the *Apollo* command module, which was perched more than 350 feet in the air atop the massive *Saturn* booster rocket. The astronauts had a long day of systems testing ahead of them, and Mission Commander Grissom grumbled about an unpleasant smell in the cockpit while technicians sealed the capsule's hatch from the outside. A simulated countdown sequence that would go on for the rest of the day was initiated. These untold hours of tedious rehearsals, run-throughs, and systems' checks in a cramped cabin were the reality behind the public's perception of the astronauts' "exciting" and "glamorous" profession.

At 6:31 P.M., biotelemetry sensors attached to astronaut White showed a dramatic increase in his heart rate and respiration. A moment later, technicians and engineers in the launch tower heard Grissom say the word *fire* over the radio. Roger Chaffee then said in a matter-of-fact manner, "We've got a fire in the cockpit." The listeners heard a burst of static over their headsets, and a Radio Corporation

The Apollo/Saturn *rocket ship during a countdown simulation on launchpad complex 39 at the Kennedy Space Center, Florida. The week-long countdown demonstration, during which all spacecraft and ground-support systems were tested, was a dress rehearsal for the actual countdown sequence.*

of America technician who was watching a bank of monitors that showed various angles of the capsule saw a bright glow through the cabin porthole; he could also see the astronauts moving about in apparent agitation. Then Chaffee's voice, no longer calm, came over the radio again: "We've got a bad fire. Let's get out. Open her up. We're burning up—" There was a scream, then silence. Technicians with fire extinguishers were already moving toward the capsule's hatch when intense flames exploded from the spacecraft, driving them back. And then, as one of the environmental control technicians who was on the scene remembered, "things just went crazy."

In the ensuing chaos it took a little more than five minutes to extinguish the flames and unseal the hatch. It seemed more like a lifetime, and for the three men trapped inside the capsule, it was. Peering in through the porthole, the would-be rescuers saw no movement at all inside the cockpit. Don Babbit, of North American Aviation (the company that built the *Apollo* command module), was the first to look inside the charred cabin. "I cannot describe what I saw" was all he could say.

Word of the disaster spread as fast as the fire had. Minutes after the fire, security guards sealed off the entire launch complex. At mission control in Houston's Manned Spacecraft Center (now the Lyndon B. Johnson Space Center), flight controllers monitoring the countdown test received a burst of garbled talk over their headsets and then the connection with Cape Canaveral was lost entirely. The controllers waited with growing dread, sensing that something terrible had occurred, and soon their fears were confirmed. Joseph Shea, the brilliant young deputy director of the Apollo Spacecraft Program Office (ASPO), was on a Florida-bound plane within the hour.

Project Apollo's top brass, including the famed rocket scientist Wernher von Braun; James Webb, NASA administrator; Robert Gilruth, head of the Space Task Group; George Mueller, head of the Office of Manned

Space Flight; and Kurt Debus, director of NASA's launch operations, were at a lively gathering at the International Club in Washington, D.C., when the phone calls started coming in. By the time most of them had managed to get to Cape Canaveral, Donald K. ("Deke") Slayton, one of the original seven Mercury astronauts and now the director of flight crew operations, was supervising the removal of the bodies from the burned command module. For NASA, the party was over.

According to Charles Murray and Catherine Bly Cox, authors of *Apollo, The Race to the Moon,* "The history of Apollo is divided into two time periods, Before the Fire and After the Fire. . . . It was not only three astronauts who died on that evening in January 1967: Some of the space program's lightheartedness and exuberance died too.

Ill-fated astronauts Virgil I. ("Gus") Grissom (left), Edward H. White (center), and Roger Chaffee (right) were scheduled to fly the first manned Apollo mission in February 1967, but a deadly flash fire swept through the cabin of the command module during a countdown test, killing the three men, on January 27, 1967.

Things had been changing all along, of course, as Apollo swelled to thousands, then tens of thousands of workers. . . . But the fire was a demarcation of the loss of innocence."

What were the origins of that time of innocence? They can be traced at least as far back as A.D. 165, when Lucian of Samosata, a Syrian, wrote A *True History*, a fanciful account of a trip to the moon. But the dream must have existed long before that; perhaps it was born, if only in the form of a vague yearning, in the mind of one of our earliest ancestors as he or she gazed with wonder at a prehistoric night sky.

When did fancy become reality? When did science fiction turn to science fact? In 1903, an amateur Russian rocket scientist named Konstantin Tsiolkovsky wrote a science fiction "novel" about spaceflight that was based on

The charred interior of the command module in which the three Apollo astronauts perished. Investigators concluded that a spark from exposed wiring started an inferno in the oxygen-rich atmosphere maintained within the cockpit. Because the hatch to the capsule was bolted shut from the outside, Grissom, White, and Chaffee could not escape.

his own research into the principles of jet propulsion. In 1926, American physicist Robert Goddard used Tsiolkovsky's theories to boost a small rocket from a makeshift launchpad in his Aunt Effie's backyard to an altitude of 41 feet. Several years later, Dr. Hermann Oberth of Romania wrote a small book about the ideas of Tsiolkovsky and Goddard called *The Rocket into Interplanetary Space*, bringing the concept of space travel via liquid-fueled rockets to the attention of scientists around the world. And by the end of World War II, Oberth and a young German colleague named Wernher von Braun were designing rockets for the Nazi war machine. When the war ended, von Braun fled to the United States, where, under the auspices of the U.S. military, he continued his work.

But for most Americans, and especially for those who would actually participate in the Apollo program, the dream became a reality on May 25, 1961, when U.S. president John F. Kennedy, in a speech to a joint session of Congress, asserted that "this nation should commit itself to achieving the goal, before this decade is out, of landing a man on the moon and returning him safely to earth." With that sentence, the president galvanized the nation and threw the combined industrial, intellectual, political, and economic weight of the United States of America behind the task of putting a human being—an American human being—on the moon. The visionary Tsiolkovsky, dreaming his rocket dreams back at the beginning of the century, would undoubtedly have smiled at the prospect, for in 1961 no nation could muster the resources that the United States could—except, perhaps, the Soviet Union.

Kennedy himself did not have much personal interest in spaceflight. His call to send an American to the moon was a propaganda ploy, generated by cold war politics. (The cold war is a term used to describe the political and economic struggle for worldwide supremacy between the United States and the Soviet Union that occurred following World War II. It was characterized by a massive

buildup of military and related technology by both na-
tions.) Along with Cuba and Berlin, where in the early
1960s disagreements between the two superpowers brought
them to the brink of war, outer space was also becoming
a cold war arena. The space race between the United States
and the Soviet Union was heating up, and the United
States was losing. The Soviet program, under the guidance
of a shadowy and daunting figure known only to Americans
as the chief designer—his name was Sergey Korolyov—
had already beaten their capitalist rivals in the race to put
a satellite and then a human being into earth orbit. *Sputnik I*, the first artificial earth satellite, was launched on
October 4, 1957; President Dwight D. Eisenhower responded to this event by forming the National Aeronautics
and Space Administration (NASA), which was charged
with the task of putting an American into space. But Yury
Gagarin, a Red Army jet-fighter pilot, became the first
human in outer space, on April 12, 1961. It was the flight
of Gagarin (along with the debacle at Cuba's Bay of Pigs,
where a U.S.-sponsored invasion failed miserably) that
prompted Kennedy to make his speech and to challenge
his countrymen to set out on what he called "the most
hazardous and dangerous and greatest adventure on which
man has ever embarked."

Thus began the period of innocence, the hopeful, op-
timistic, we-can-do-anything era for NASA and Project
Apollo. For if Kennedy's motivations were political, the
motivations of the men and women who answered his call
and formed the core of the Apollo program were pure.
They were the best and the brightest of American technological minds, the heirs to the legacy of the Wright
brothers: artists of aerodynamic design, builders of rockets
and rocket engines, specialists in the physics of the upper
atmosphere, makers of new alloys, experimenters in py-
rotechnics, innovators in radio communication and telem-
etry, creators of artificial environments, geologists of the
extraterrestrial, manipulators of gravity. From all over

America and from outside the country as well, they answered Kennedy's call. (Many of these people came from
the private sector—from universities and aeronautics cor-
porations—but most of the original Apollo personnel, such
as von Braun and his rocket men, had been part of American army, navy, and air force missile and satellite research
and development projects that had been absorbed by NASA

*Pioneer cosmonaut Yury Gagarin,
the first human being in outer
space. Gagarin, a 27-year-old
Red Air Force fighter pilot, orbited
the earth in* Vostok 1 *on April 12,
1961, giving the Soviet Union
a head start in the space race.*

President John F. Kennedy reacted to the news of Yury Gagarin's historic spaceflight by addressing a joint session of Congress on May 25, 1961. During his speech, Kennedy challenged the nation to put an American on the moon by the end of the decade—and before the Soviets.

when it was formed in 1958.) Congress responded as well, providing NASA with the necessary funding. (Project Apollo would eventually cost about $25 billion.)

At various NASA facilities around the country, work on Apollo began. At a place in Hampton, Virginia, known to NASA personnel as Langley (its official title was the Samuel P. Langley Memorial Aeronautical Laboratory), a brilliant young engineer named Maxime Faget began experimenting with prototype designs for the gumdrop-shaped capsule that would become the *Apollo* command module (CM). He was assisted by a gifted aeronautical designer and draftsman named Caldwell Johnson. At the air force missile facility at Cape Canaveral, Florida, Kurt Debus and Rocco Petrone began the truly monumental task of building a launch system. At the Marshall Space Center in Huntsville, Alabama, Wernher von Braun's team began work on the enormous *Saturn* booster, the world's largest and most powerful rocket. In 1961, the Manned Spacecraft Center was opened in Houston. It would become the home of mission control and the hub of the ever-growing NASA operations. And as the Apollo program expanded, administrators and departmental leaders emerged. These were the men who would keep Project Apollo on course and steer it safely through a succession of technological, financial, political, logistical, and moral crises—men such as Robert Gilruth, Joseph Shea, Christopher C. Kraft, Jr., George Low, James E. Webb, and George Mueller.

At first, the developers of Project Apollo were faced with a bewildering array of questions, choices, and decisions. Perhaps the single most important choice that had to be made during the early days of Apollo was the "mode decision"—the exact manner in which the astronauts might leave the earth, fly to the moon, land on it, and then return. There were many different ways to approach this scenario. Although, as Caldwell Johnson put it, "we had more harebrained schemes than you could shake a stick at," NASA quickly narrowed it down to three possible modes: direct approach, earth orbit rendezvous (EOR), or lunar orbit rendezvous (LOR).

The direct-approach mode involved flying a huge, self-contained ship to the moon, landing it there, and then flying it back to earth. This would require a booster rocket of unprecedented proportions—a gargantuan thing tentatively called the *Nova* that probably could not be built and perfected before Kennedy's end-of-the-decade deadline. The earth-orbit-rendezvous mode involved two separate launches of smaller, more feasible boosters; one would carry the lunar spacecraft into earth orbit, and the other would carry a fuel tank into earth orbit. During rendez-vous, the lunar spacecraft would be fueled, after which it would fly to the moon, land, and return. This mode would be difficult and dangerous, but the majority of Apollo engineers agreed that it was more workable, under the time limitations, than the direct-approach mode. Finally, there was the lunar-orbit-rendezvous mode. In this sce-nario, a single launch would propel the lunar spacecraft to the moon, where it would go into orbit. Then, a small, separate craft—it would come to be known as the lunar module, or LM—would break free from the mother ship, land on the moon, and then rejoin the mother ship in lunar orbit for the journey home.

At first, the LOR mode was viewed as something of a crackpot scheme. It seemed too complicated and too dan-gerous. As program chief George Low put it, "LOR in-volved doing a rendezvous a quarter of a million miles from home. It seemed like an extremely far-out thing to do." But a Langley engineer named John Houbolt was convinced that LOR was the way to go. For Houbolt, LOR seemed simpler and more economical. It eliminated the need for the direct-approach superbooster and the EOR multiple launches and earth-orbit rendezvous. With LOR, the entire launch package would be lighter, because the tiny LM would not need as much fuel to land and then take off from the moon as the much larger direct-approach or EOR craft would. And the LM could be discarded after the lunar landing and the rendezvous with the mother ship was completed; thus, because it was that much lighter, less fuel would be needed for the mother ship's return journey.

Houbolt waged a one-man campaign for the lunar-orbit mode. "It became clear," he wrote later, "that lunar-orbit rendezvous offered a chain-reaction simplification [of all the aspects of the mission to the moon]: development, testing, manufacturing, erection, countdown, flight op-erations etc." Gradually, Apollo engineers began to see

German scientist Wernher von Braun is dwarfed by the F-1 engines that would power the first stage of the Saturn booster. The Saturn was the ultimate realization of the interplanetary visions of von Braun's youth, when he first experimented with small liquid-fueled rockets in a wooded area near Berlin.

merit in the idea, although a hard core of resistance remained among some of the more influential figures, including von Braun and Faget. A decision was finally pushed through by Joe Shea, ASPO deputy director. Shea recognized the importance of making the decision, one way or another—the Apollo program was at a virtual standstill and could go no further until the mode issue was cleared up. And Shea was tough; he did not mind stepping on some toes or ruffling some feathers, as long as the issue

(continued on page 26)

"Any Shape It Wanted to Be"

During the breathless days leading up to the *Apollo 11* mission, the lunar module, or LM (pronounced "lem"), attracted more attention than any other component of the Apollo spacecraft. Newspapers, magazines, and television shows in countries around the world featured the LM, which was built by the Grumman Engineering Corporation; children especially were attracted to the vehicle. Part of the reason for this was the role the LM would play—it was the flying machine that would actually transport the astronauts down to the surface of the moon. But the main reason for the public's fascination with the LM was its appearance. A squat, ungainly four-legged pod, the LM looked like nothing so much as a big metallic insect, and the designers and engineers at NASA and Grumman referred to it, quite appropriately, as "the bug."

Why was the LM so odd looking? The explanation was simple. Because it would fly only in the vacuum of outer space—rather than in both outer space and the earth's atmosphere, like the *Saturn* booster and the command-service module—its designers did not have to worry about any aerodynamic factors. Therefore, as one designer put it, the LM could be "any shape it wanted to be. It didn't have to be round-edged and smooth. It could be square. It could have corners on it. Things could stick out at odd angles." Designers and engineers accustomed to creating aircraft that were streamlined to deal with the stresses and strains of the earth's thick atmosphere adopted a new design philosophy. Suitable to the aerodynamic void of outer space, this new guiding principle was called "functional asymmetry," and it resulted in the whimsical appearance—and successful performance—of the Apollo LM.

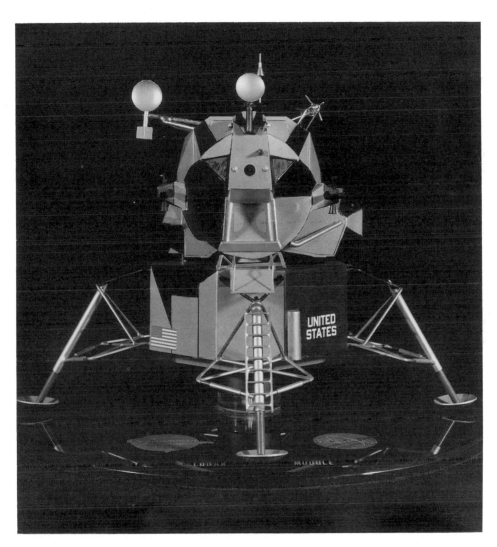

An early model of the Apollo lunar module, built by the Grumman Engineering Corporation of Bethpage, Long Island.

(continued from page 23)

was settled. Between Shea's administrative pressure and Houbolt's engineering advocacy, LOR finally won out. In June 1962, von Braun admitted that LOR "offers the highest confidence factor of successful accomplishment within this decade."

With the mode controversy out of the way, Project Apollo gained momentum. Independent contractors were chosen to manufacture thousands of components, from the massive to the minuscule. North American Aviation (now Rockwell International) would build the mother ship—the command module and the service module, or CSM. Rocketdyne Corporation was chosen to construct the rocket engines that would power the *Saturn* booster. And Grumman Engineering Corporation won the contract

Kurt Debus, NASA's director of launch operations, monitors lift-off preparations in the firing room at the Kennedy Space Center. Along with the astronauts, scientists, and engineers who responded to Kennedy's call to put an American on the moon were administrators such as Debus, who organized and managed the unwieldy NASA infrastructure.

for the lunar module. In the meantime, the space race continued.

During the early sixties it seemed clear that the Soviets were winning the race. NASA's Mercury program had matched the Soviet accomplishments of putting a man in space and then into earth orbit (Alan Shepard was the first American in space, May 5, 1961; John Glenn was the first to orbit the earth, February 20, 1962), but Chief Designer Korolyov had kept his Vostok and then Voskhod programs consistently one step ahead of NASA. Korolyov beat NASA to all the earth-orbit firsts: The Soviets were the first to put a man in space (Yury Gagarin, *Vostok 1*, April 12, 1961); the first to put a man in orbit (Gagarin, *Vostok 1*); the first to achieve a double launch and flight (*Vostok 3 and 4*, August 1962); the first to put a woman in orbit (Valentina Tereshkova, *Vostok 6*, June 1963); the first to achieve a multiple-passenger flight (*Voskhod 1*, October 1964); and the first to undertake extravehicular activity (EVA), more commonly known as a space walk (Aleksei Leonov, *Voskhod 2*, March 18, 1965.)

But things began to change as NASA's Gemini program got under way. NASA intended to use Gemini to develop and perfect the various techniques and the associated hardware that would be needed to reach the moon via the LOR mode. During Gemini, which had its first manned flight in March 1965 (*Gemini 3*, piloted by Gus Grissom and John W. Young), NASA investigated and developed orbital rendezvous and docking techniques, multiple-passenger and long-duration spaceflight procedures, and EVA techniques. The Gemini program was wildly successful. After the final *Gemini* capsule splashed down safely on November 15, 1966, confidence was running high at NASA. The first manned Project Apollo launch was scheduled for February 21, 1967. Kennedy's deadline seemed within reach. Then, on January 27, 1967, astronauts Grissom, White, and Chaffee climbed into the command module for a countdown test.

After the Fire

Apollo 7 *insignia*

Considering the nature of the disaster that befell *Apollo 1*, it would not have been surprising if the entire Apollo program had been derailed or even scrubbed permanently. Although the exact origin of the fire could not be determined, a congressional investigation, as well as NASA's own investigation into the incident, revealed numerous safety hazards, most of them related to faulty wiring. The two primary culprits in the death of the astronauts were the 100-percent-oxygen atmosphere that was maintained within the spacecraft and the hatch that was bolted shut from the outside. A high-oxygen atmosphere is extremely volatile; investigators surmised that a spark from some exposed wiring had quickly become an inferno. And because the hatch was bolted from the outside, the astronauts could not get it open in time to escape.

Following the fire, NASA came under considerable pressure from Congress, the press, and the public, but it weathered the storm. Many NASA people even believed that the fire had strengthened the program in certain ways, despite the terrible cost. Joe Shea referred to the fire and the ensuing controversy as a "crucible" and a "unifying force." (Shea himself retired from NASA following the fire and was replaced by George Low.) Another NASA engineer said that "from an overall standpoint of the program, it might have been one of the best things that could

Astronaut Walter M. Schirra undergoes pressure-suit adjustments prior to the October 1968 lift-off of Apollo 7, *NASA's first attempt at a manned flight following the* Apollo 1 *tragedy. Schirra's expression conveys the tension that surrounded the mission; the future of Project Apollo depended on a successful flight.*

*President Lyndon B. Johnson
presents the flag that covered the
casket of astronaut Gus Grissom
to his widow, Betty Grissom,
following funeral services at
Arlington National Cemetery
January 31, 1967. For
Americans, the deaths of Grissom
and fellow astronauts White and
Chaffee were a frightening
reminder of the risks involved in
manned space exploration.*

have happened. I think we got too complacent in the program. . . . The fire really woke people up." The astronauts themselves reacted to the fire with characteristic test-pilot stoicism. All of them knew the risks involved and accepted them. Their attitude was expressed by Grissom himself shortly before the fire: "The conquest of space is worth the risk of life."

It was thus a less innocent but more hardened, determined, and focused NASA that emerged from the fire. Unmanned tests—*Apollo 4, Apollo 5,* and *Apollo 6*—of the *Apollo/Saturn* vehicle were completed by early 1968.

Despite a series of nagging problems that included fuel spills and computer, booster-engine, and LM-engine malfunctions, NASA went ahead with plans for a manned test flight.

Apollo 7, an earth-orbit test flight of the redesigned command-service module, began on October 11, 1968. (The service module was connected directly to the command module and contained its own propulsion system, the spacecraft's oxygen and hydrogen tanks, and the main fuel cells.) It was the most crucial event yet in the short lifetime of NASA and the Apollo program, for the *Apollo 1* tragedy was still fresh in everybody's mind and the entire world was watching. NASA's credibility and the future of the Apollo program were at stake. Throughout the next 11 days, audiences on earth watched live earth-orbit television. Aside from a series of minor technical glitches and the head colds that afflicted the crew—Walter Schirra, Don Eisele, and R. Walter Cunningham—*Apollo 7* was a success, and the men and women of NASA uncrossed their fingers and breathed a sigh of relief.

The next mission, *Apollo 8*, was scheduled for a December launch. *Apollo 8* had been planned as a manned test for the lunar module in earth orbit, but George Low, deputy director of ASPO, had another idea. Learning that the LM would not be ready for a December launch, Low, rather than postpone the mission, proposed a manned, round-trip lunar flight for *Apollo 8*. This was an extremely nervy proposition. Many people, inside and outside NASA, were not quite sure that the Apollo program was ready for such a flight. But Low's reasoning was sound. Why cancel an entire mission just because the LM was not ready? A successful circumlunar (around the moon) flight would represent a quantum leap for Project Apollo. If the mission was successful, the momentum generated would put to rest once and for all any lingering doubts about the program, and it would also finally give NASA an undisputed edge in the race with the Soviets, who had

Apollo 8 *insignia*

Apollo 7 *astronauts Donald Eisele and Walter Schirra (second and third from left) enjoy breakfast with NASA officials at the Kennedy Space Center during preparations for their mission. Apollo 7, an 11-day earth-orbital flight, was completed without mishap on October 22, 1968.*

recently achieved an unmanned circumlunar flight (*Zond* 5, September 1968).

A manned circumlunar flight was a gamble at that point—a serious problem or mishap of any sort might deal a fatal blow to the Apollo program. But Low was convinced that it was a good gamble, and soon he had a groundswell of support at NASA. His main obstacle was the top man, NASA administrator James Webb, but Webb cleared the way when he resigned in October. He was replaced by

Thomas Paine, who gave his approval for an *Apollo* 8 circumlunar mission.

Apollo 8 was probably the best gamble ever taken by NASA. Manned by astronauts Frank Borman, James A. Lovell, Jr., and William A. Anders, *Apollo* 8 was launched from Cape Canaveral on December 21, 1968. Within days, these space explorers had traveled farther away from the earth than any humans before them. Early on the morning of December 24, *Apollo* 8 looped around the far side of the moon. The spacecraft orbited the moon 10 times while the 3 earthlings got the first live, close-up look

Apollo 8 *lunar-module pilot William Anders (left), command-module pilot James Lovell, Jr. (center), and Mission Commander Frank Borman practice in the Apollo simulator. NASA astronauts spent hundreds of hours inside flight simulators before their missions; it was the most essential part of their training.*

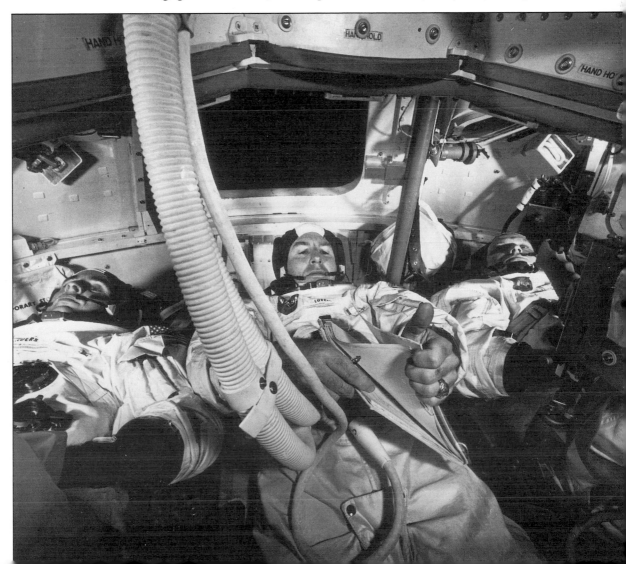

Apollo 9 *insignia*

Apollo 10 *insignia*

at the object that passed nightly across their home skies, once so far away and yet now so close. Borman described it as a "vast, lonely, and forbidding sight." On Christmas morning, *Apollo 8* completed its final orbit and headed for home. The command module splashed down safely on December 27, about 1,100 miles southwest of Hawaii. Helicopters quickly retrieved the astronauts from the floating spacecraft and flew them to the aircraft carrier USS *Yorktown*, waiting a scant 5,000 yards away.

Apollo 8 was a watershed mission for NASA's lunar program. It also sounded the death knell for the faltering Soviet moon effort. Like NASA, the Soviet program had suffered a fatal accident in 1967. The highly respected cosmonaut Vladimir Komarov was killed on April 24, 1967, when his *Soyuz 1* spacecraft crash-landed in the Ural Mountains of Central Asia. In spite of this, the Soviets continued to press forward with their Zond, Soyuz, and Kosmos lunar programs, believing, or perhaps simply hoping, that NASA was not yet ready to make an attempt at a lunar landing. They found out that they were quite wrong about this when *Apollo 8* circumnavigated the moon in December 1968. Subsequent problems with the Zond's *Proton* booster eliminated any hope the Soviets might still have harbored to beat their rivals to the moon, and they dropped out of the race.

NASA wanted to make two more flights before attempting a lunar landing. *Apollo 9*, an earth-orbit flight, was launched on March 3, 1969. After *Apollo 8*, this mission seemed anticlimactic, but it was critical to a successful lunar landing, being the first manned test during one flight of all the major Apollo components, including the LM. The mission, piloted by James A. McDivitt, David R. Scott, and Russel L. Schweickart, ended on March 13 and was deemed a success.

The next step, *Apollo 10*, was a final dress rehearsal before committing astronauts to a lunar-landing attempt. *Apollo 10* would include lunar-orbit tests of the CSM and the LM and a close lunar flyby for the purpose of surface reconnaissance, during which photographs of the proposed landing site would be taken. *Apollo 10* was launched on May 18; on May 21, astronauts Thomas P. Stafford, Eugene A. Cernan, and John W. Young made two close passes over the targeted landing site for *Apollo 11*. As the *Apollo 10* spacecraft swooped down low over the pockmarked lunar surface, the astronauts and everybody in NASA realized that the moon was now within reach. Eugene Cernan's exhilarated remarks to mission control at that point summed up the feelings of everybody involved in Project Apollo. "We're right there!" he exclaimed. "We're right over it! I'm telling you, we are low, we're close, babe."

One of the more important aspects of Apollo 9 *was the testing of the lunar module for the first time in outer space. In this photo, taken with planet earth in the background, the odd-looking lunar module—this one was appropriately nicknamed Spider—deploys its landing gear. Lunar surface probes extend down from the footpads. NASA hoped that this misshapen pod would ferry astronauts from the mother ship to the moon and back.*

Sea of Tranquility

Apollo 11 *insignia*

Two simple words forever changed the lives of Neil Armstrong, Buzz Aldrin, and Mike Collins, securing for them a special niche in the history of the human race. On January 6, 1969, director of flight-crew operations Deke Slayton confronted the three astronauts and without ceremony told them, "You're it." Armstrong, Aldrin, and Collins did not have to ask Slayton to clarify his statement, for they knew exactly what he meant—they were going to the moon.

Apollo 11 mission commander Neil Aldin Armstrong, destined to become the most famous of all the astronauts and cosmonauts, was cut from the same basic cloth as the American men who had preceded him into outer space. Born the son of a state tax auditor on an Ohio farm in 1930, Armstrong was obsessed with flying even as a little boy, when he often dreamed that he could float around like a balloon by holding his breath. He had his pilot's license by the age of 16. Armstrong left Purdue University during his second year and became a navy fighter pilot; he flew 78 combat missions in the Korean War.

When the war was over, Armstrong did something that would set him apart from his future colleagues in the astronaut corps—he left the armed forces. (Armstrong would be NASA's first civilian astronaut.) Returning to Purdue, he obtained a degree in aeronautical engineering and married his longtime sweetheart Jan Shearson. Soon

Man on the moon: Apollo 11 lunar-module pilot Edwin E. ("Buzz") Aldrin, Jr., with the LM looming behind him, deploys part of a solar wind detector in the Sea of Tranquility, July 20, 1969. The photograph was taken by Mission Commander Neil Armstrong—the first human to walk on the moon.

after, he became a test pilot for NASA. At Edwards Air Force Base in California, Armstrong was paid to check out the newest, fastest, and most dangerous high-performance aircraft being developed at that time, including volatile rocket planes such as the X-15. He was selected as an astronaut in 1962 and piloted the *Gemini* 8 mission in March 1966.

Why was Neil Armstrong given command of the *Apollo 11* mission, the most important flight since Orville Wright piloted the flimsy *Kitty Hawk* into history back in 1903? He was widely regarded as one of the best pilots in the astronaut corps, but there was more to it than that. Armstrong projected an air of unassailable competence and confidence. Words such as *stoic, imperturbable*, and *unflappable* and phrases like "ice water in his veins" are usually used to describe him. (Some of his colleagues even found him cool to the point of inscrutability and felt that he was unapproachable on a personal level.) The ability to function effectively in a crisis was a paramount requirement for a spaceflight mission commander, and Armstrong had displayed this quality on numerous occasions. The most memorable example of Armstrong's ability to remain cool under pressure (prior to *Apollo 11*) was his performance during the *Gemini* 8 flight, when a jammed thruster caused the orbiting CM to go into a rapid tumble. Armstrong displayed an almost preternatural calm in handling this potentially disastrous situation, and that more than anything else made him the prime candidate for *Apollo 11* mission commander. It would prove to be a fateful and wise choice for NASA.

Edwin Eugene "Buzz" Aldrin, Jr., the *Apollo 11* LM pilot, was born in Montclair, New Jersey, in 1930. His father was an air force colonel, and Buzz seemed destined to be a pilot and a lunar astronaut—his mother's maiden name was Moon. Aldrin graduated third in his class from West Point and then went to fly air force fighter jets in the Korean conflict, where he terrorized Chinese MiG

Neil Armstrong speaks with technicians after donning his pressure suit on Apollo 11 *launch day, July 16, 1969. Soon after this photo was taken, Armstrong's helmet was fastened on, enclosing him in a 100-percent-oxygen atmosphere.*

pilots. After the war, he obtained a Ph.D. in engineering. Aldrin was one of NASA's premier orbital-rendezvous experts—his nickname was Dr. Rendezvous. His first space-flight was *Gemini 12* in 1966, during which he made a record five-and-a-half-hour spacewalk.

Aldrin was a different sort of astronaut, especially when compared to the sanguine Armstrong. A sensitive man of a more philosophical nature than Armstrong, Aldrin battled depression both before and after the lunar mission. He had an active imagination, which could be a curse for astronauts, who were often confronted with a reality that was already overwhelming in its strangeness and danger. There is something intrinsically human in Aldrin's story; the events of *Apollo 11* make Armstrong seem like a superhero, whereas the troubled Aldrin seems ordinary, a mere man, with doubts and fears and dashed hopes just like any other earthling (he had wished desperately to be the first astronaut to walk on the moon and was bitterly

Buzz Aldrin in a photograph taken by Neil Armstrong inside the Eagle. *Aldrin, as LM pilot, would accompany Armstrong during the attempt to land the* Eagle *on the moon.*

disappointed when Armstrong was given that privilege). Because of his inner conflicts, it might be said that Aldrin had to muster a different and more rare form of courage than many of the other astronauts.

Although Michael Collins, the 39-year-old CM pilot for *Apollo 11*, was born in Rome, Italy, he was truly an all-American boy. Collins was the son of a respected army general. He graduated from West Point and became an air force fighter pilot, and in 1963 he was selected by NASA for astronaut training. In 1966 he was part of the *Gemini 10* crew. Youthful and enthusiastic but also perceptive, cautious, and realistic, he formed the perfect complement to the laconic Armstrong and the intense and somewhat irreverent Aldrin.

These three men were awakened just after four o'clock on the morning of July 16, 1969. They were quartered in the manned spacecraft operations building, located about eight miles from the Cape Canaveral launch site where the towering *Apollo 11* rocket ship waited for them. After a cursory physical examination by a NASA nurse, they showered, shaved, and ate a final earth breakfast of steak, eggs, toast, coffee, and orange juice. After breakfast, they went upstairs to the suit room. Biotelemetry electrodes that would allow mission control to monitor heart rate and respiration were attached to their chests, and then NASA technicians helped them into their pressure suits and helmets. Once they were all sealed into the artificial, 100 percent oxygen atmosphere of the suits, they trooped clumsily back downstairs and out to the van that would transfer them to the launchpad.

Although more than a million spectators crowded the beaches and highways around the Kennedy Space Center, the route to the launchpad was cleared by police, and the astronauts' ride took only a few minutes. Sealed inside their suits, Armstrong, Aldrin, and Collins were alone with their thoughts at that point, their eyes peering out from

Apollo 11 *command-module pilot Michael Collins practices rendezvous and docking maneuvers in the CM simulator. Although Collins would not get to walk on the moon—he would pilot the* Columbia *in lunar orbit while Armstrong and Aldrin landed on the surface—his contribution to the mission was vital.*

behind the visors of their helmets at the rocket. As the van brought them closer and closer, the *Apollo/Saturn* loomed larger and larger. It was an awesome sight, the culmination of nine years of intensive research and development. The *Apollo/Saturn* rocket ship in its entirety, from the ground up, consisted of the three-stage *Saturn V* booster; atop the uppermost, third stage, inside a special adaptor, was the lunar module *Eagle*; atop the *Eagle* was the command-service module (the mother ship) *Columbia*; and atop the *Columbia*, at the very tip of this 363-foot arrow, was the launch escape system, a small rocket that would pull the command module and astronauts away from the rest of the assembly in the event of a catastrophic launch occurrence.

An elevator in the umbilical tower brought the three men to the top of the booster and they laboriously assumed their seats in the cramped cockpit of the command module *Columbia*. Soon after, the astronauts' isolation was ended as they were put into radio contact with launch and flight controllers and with one another. The CM hatch was slammed shut and sealed. (Unlike the *Apollo 1* hatch, this one could be opened quickly from within in the event of an emergency.) Armstrong, Collins, and Aldrin spent the next two hours completing a final systems' check as the countdown to launch proceeded without interruption.

Lift-off occurred at 9:32 P.M.. For those who had come to Florida to witness the launch in person, it was a fiery, thunderous, earth-shaking experience—even from 10 miles away. Inside the CM cockpit, there was, in the words of Mike Collins, "noise, yes, lots of it, but mostly motion, as we are thrown left and right against our straps in spasmodic little jerks." The first two of the *Saturn*'s three stages used up their fuel and were discarded; the final stage pushed the *Apollo 11* CSM into earth orbit and then shut down. Eleven minutes and 42 seconds had elapsed since lift-off.

Apollo 11 was now orbiting the earth at an altitude of roughly 100 miles and a speed of 18,000 miles per hour.

About halfway through the second orbit, translunar injection (TLI) was initiated. This was the final, crucial firing of the remaining stage of the *Saturn* booster; the TLI burn (a "burn" was a timed firing of a rocket engine in flight) would allow the spacecraft to achieve escape velocity—25,000 MPH—and thus break free from earth orbit. *Apollo 11*'s TLI was successful, boosting the spacecraft out of earth orbit and giving it a final push toward the moon. Three hours had passed since lift-off and the spacecraft was now, in the words of Collins, "climbing like a dingbat."

But it was not yet time for the astronauts to relax. Another important and tricky maneuver was at hand—transposition and docking. This procedure would transform the remaining components of the *Apollo/Saturn* vehicle into the LOR-mode spacecraft first envisioned back in the days when Apollo engineers were trying to figure out how best to fly men to the moon, land them on the lunar surface,

The mission control room at the Manned Spacecraft Center, Houston, Texas. For every astronaut who flew to the moon, there were thousands of people on earth who played a crucial part in the mission. "Hell, you can't get along without them" was one astronaut's assessment of NASA's support personnel.

and return them safely to earth. Collins, as command module pilot, would handle the transposition and docking. First, Collins detached the CSM *Columbia* from the remaining stage of the *Saturn* booster, which carried the spacecraft lunar adaptor. The adaptor housed the lunar module *Eagle*, which was, in Collins's words, "nestled in its container atop the Saturn like a mechanical tarantula crouched in its hole." Once he had separated the CSM from the *Saturn* and LM, Collins, using small maneuvering thrusters, flew the CSM about 75 feet away from the *Saturn* and executed a 180 degree turn so that the nose probe of the CSM was now facing the top of the *Saturn* and where the LM nested. Then, deftly manipulating the handles controlling the maneuvering thrusters—it must be remembered that the CSM and the *Saturn* were hurtling along together at upwards of 2,000 MPH during this process—Collins effected the docking, moving the CSM forward until its nose slipped into a drogue atop the LM. There was a slight bang as Collins nudged the CSM nose into the LM drogue, and then the two vehicles locked together as one. Finally, the third stage of the *Saturn*, the LM's former host, was jettisoned. The astronauts would now rely on the service module's engine (the service propulsion system), as well as the gravitational influences of the earth, sun, and moon, to get them to the moon and back.

The astronauts could now relax. They were entering cislunar space, the empty reaches between the earth and the moon, utterly black except for the streaks of perpetual sunlight. The men took off their uncomfortable pressure suits and settled in for the trip across the void. (NASA mission rules required the astronauts to keep their pressure suits and helmets on until after transposition and docking in case of an accidental loss of cabin pressure during the rough launch, ascent, TLI, and transposition and docking sequences.) The moon is roughly 237,000 miles away from the earth, depending on its orbital position; Armstrong, Collins, and Aldrin had more than 2 full days of cislunar travel ahead of them. They passed the time with mundane but essential housekeeping duties; with eating, sleeping, thinking, and communicating with mission control; with monitoring the spacecraft's trajectory and navigational systems; and with watching planet earth grow smaller and smaller as they left it behind. It shrank steadily, as an astronaut on a later mission recalled, "from the size of a basketball down to the size of a baseball, then a golf ball, then finally the size of a marble."

Early on the fourth day, the spacecraft passed the equigravisphere—the point where the earth's gravitational pull gives way to the moon's. *Columbia's* speed increased dramatically as the moon pulled it toward the lunar center of gravity; the spacecraft was, in effect, falling into the moon, which grew larger in the windows by the minute. "The moon I have known all my life," Collins later wrote, "that two-dimensional, small yellow disk in the sky, has gone away somewhere, to be replaced by the most awesome sphere I have ever seen. . . . It is *huge*, completely filling our window."

The cislunar coast was almost over and now the astronauts prepared for the next crucial firing of the CSM engine—lunar orbit insertion one (LOI-1). Lunar orbit insertion one was actually a braking maneuver, or, in the words of Collins, "a procedure for slowing down enough" to be drawn into lunar orbit. The duration of the LOI-1 burn had to be exact: If the engine fired for too long, the spacecraft would slow down too much and succumb completely to the moon's gravitational pull, crashing onto the lunar surface. But if the LOI-1 burn was too short, the spacecraft would not be slowed enough and would shoot past the moon and keep going—forever.

Apollo 11's LOI-1 burn was near perfect. "That was a beautiful burn," Armstrong reported to mission control. Next came the LOI-2 burn, which lowered the *Columbia* into a circular orbit with an altitude of 60 miles. Collins, Armstrong, and Aldrin studied the lunar surface as they circled the moon again and again. They were particularly

anxious to get a look at the proposed landing site for the
LM in the Sea of Tranquility. (This "sea" was one of the
moon's *maria*: large, flat, desertlike plains that looked, to
the astronomers who named them, like bodies of water.)
Collins did not like the look of the moonscape, finding it
"distinctly forbidding" and "stark and barren." As the *Columbia* continued to orbit, the astronauts settled down to
sleep. Tomorrow was lunar-landing day.

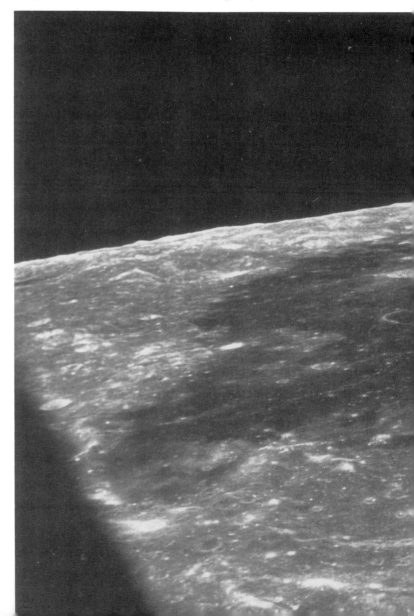

Preparations for the attempted lunar landing began as soon as the three men awoke. Armstrong and Aldrin donned their pressure suits (the astronauts called them moon cocoons) and then crawled through the 30-inch-diameter connecting tunnel into the *Eagle*. Standing at the controls (the LM had no seats), they began preparing the craft for separation from the mother ship *Columbia* and for the descent to the Sea of Tranquility.

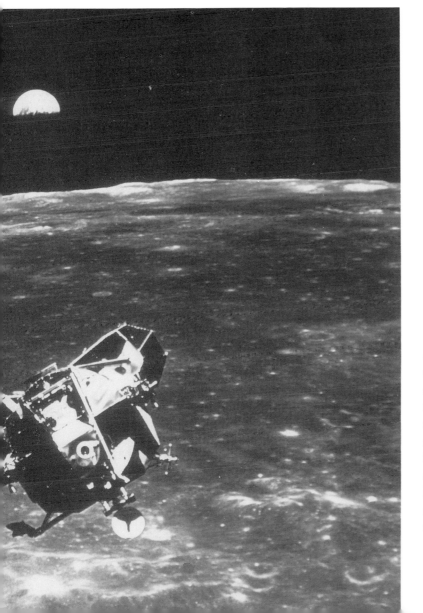

As the earth rises above the moon's horizon, the LM Eagle's ascent stage approaches the mother ship Columbia *for rendezvous and docking following the successful lunar landing. Once Armstrong and Aldrin were back on board the* Columbia, *the LM would be jettisoned and left behind to eventually crash onto the moon's surface.*

The *Eagle* undocked from the *Columbia* at 1:46 P.M. Collins, now alone in the *Columbia*, circled the LM like a worried mother, inspecting the craft to make sure everything looked as it should. Then, with a plaintive farewell—"You guys take care"—Collins maneuvered away, and the *Eagle* began its precipitous descent. Collins had an unenviable task ahead of him. Locked in an anxious lunar orbit, he could do nothing for the next 24 hours but monitor communications between mission control and the *Eagle* and pray that nothing went wrong with the lunar landing. If something happened to the *Eagle* and it was unable to lift off from the lunar surface, which was a distinct possibility, Collins would have a long, lonely flight back to earth without his friends.

Something disastrous very nearly did happen. As the odd-looking LM lowered itself down toward the lunar surface, alarms indicating a computer overload began to go off. Simultaneously, Armstrong and mission control realized that the *Eagle*'s landing trajectory was incorrect. In Houston, mission-control guidance officer Steve Bales was faced with a crucial, split-second decision—to abort the landing (and thus the entire mission, for they had fuel enough for one attempt only) or to give the astronauts the go-ahead despite the problem with the LM's guidance computer. Bales, "on instinct," he later confessed, gave Armstrong permission to attempt the landing.

This was what Armstrong and Aldrin wanted to hear. But the two astronauts now found themselves between a rock and a hard place. The computer malfunction had caused them to overshoot the intended landing site, and they were rapidly running out of fuel. Now Armstrong proved that his reputation as a pilot with steel nerves was well founded. As the LM sank lower and lower and the fuel began to run dry—at 30 feet above the lunar surface the LM had only 30 seconds of fuel remaining—Armstrong calmly found a good landing area among the boulders and craters and set the LM gently down on the moon.

(continued on page 57)

Moon Shots

The destination

Project Apollo was the most collective of exploratory ventures. The task of putting an astronaut on the moon required the efforts and resources of an entire society, from the factory workers who assembled parts for the Apollo spacecraft to the physicists who calculated the coordinates for a lunar-orbit rendezvous between those same vehicles. The media, and the visual media in particular, played a major role as well. Setting up and operating television cameras and taking still photographs were activities that were given high priority throughout Project Apollo, and rightfully so, for each camera represented the eyes of science—and the eyes of the world. But the cameras did not function as solely informational instruments. The glorious, fiery launch of a Saturn rocket; the delicate, zero-gravity ballet of two spacecraft about to dock; an astronaut moving across the bleak lunar surface; earthrise as viewed from the Ocean of Storms; these otherworldly sights, captured on film, are distinctly attractive to the human eye. The resulting outer-space aesthetic, adopted by painters, photographers, and especially filmmakers the world over, has had a profound and lasting effect on commercial and popular art in the late 20th century; thus, the cameras of Project Apollo yielded something more than a simple visual record.

Lift-off, Apollo 16, *April 16*, 1972.

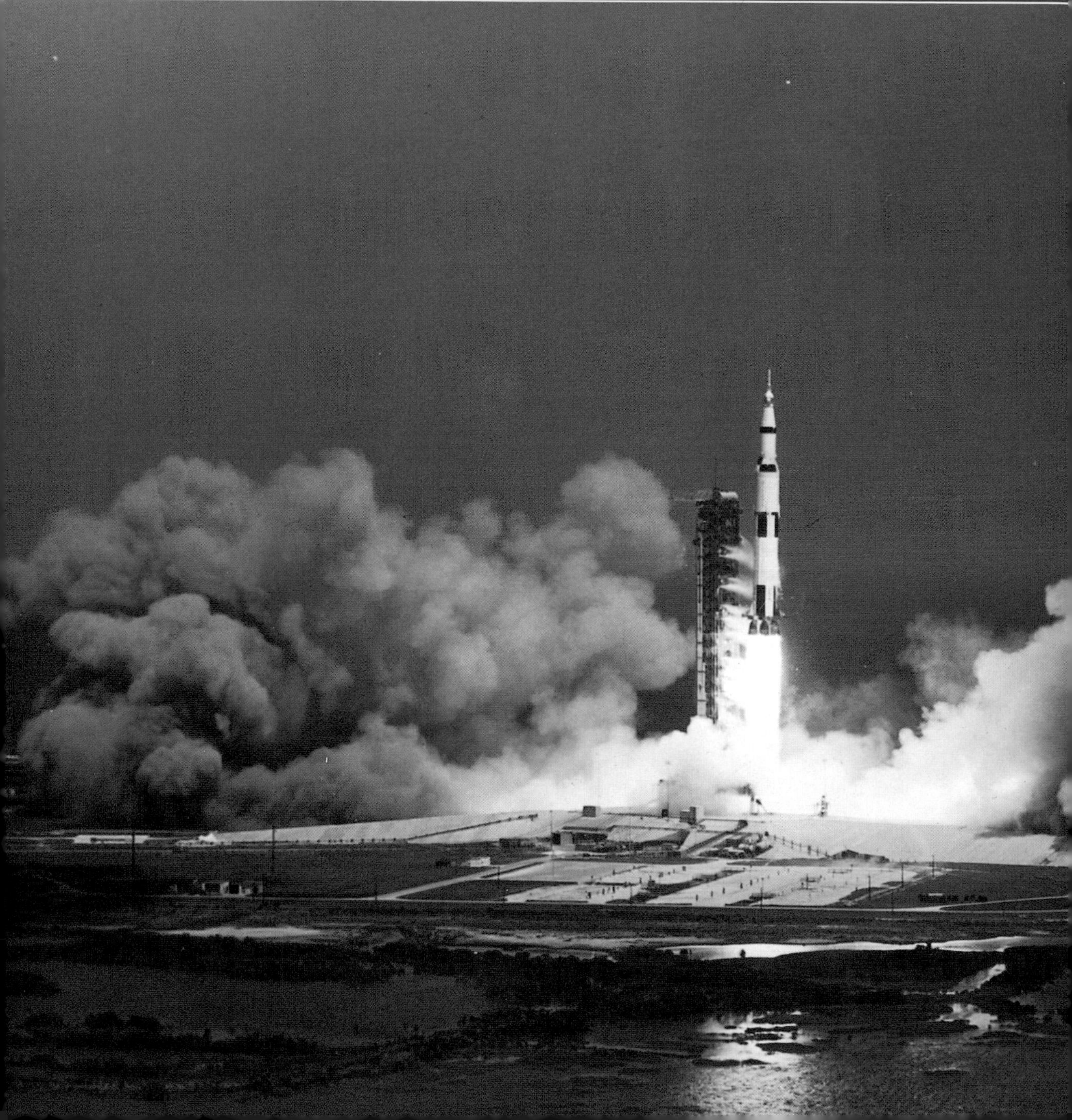

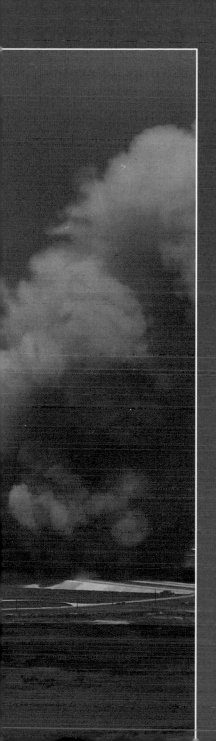

Lift-off, Apollo 13, April 11, 1970.

Lunar module Intrepid *begins descent to the Ocean of Storms, November 17, 1969.*

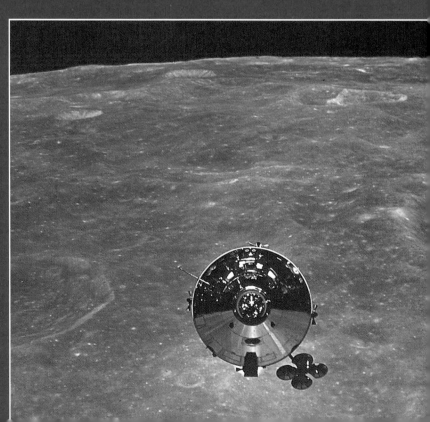

Command module Charlie Brown *in lunar orbit, May 1969.*

Apollo astronaut and the lunar rover in the Hadley-Apennine region, August 1971.

Lunar module Falcon, *astronaut David Scott, and the lunar rover at the edge of Hadley Rille, August 1971.*

Astronaut Harrison H. Schmitt and the lunar rover in the Taurus-Littrow region, December 1972.

Earthrise and the return of the lunar module Eagle, *July 21, 1969.*

(continued from page 49)

Armstrong and Aldrin looked at one another and grinned. In mission control, there was dead silence as everyone waited and listened. Finally, they heard Armstrong's voice over the radio: "Houston, Tranquility Base here. The *Eagle* has landed." A wild celebration erupted in the mission control room. In the LM cockpit, Armstrong and Aldrin reached across the instrument panel and shook hands silently. It was 4:18 P.M., July 20, 1969.

The New York Times *trumpets the astounding news, July 21, 1969.*

Ocean of Storms

Apollo 12 *insignia*

"The surface is fine and powdery. . . . I can see the footprints of my boots . . . in the fine sandy particles." This description came to the earth from the surface of the moon, where Neil Armstrong was standing. Not long before, he had stepped down from the LM onto the moon, uttering the famous words—"One small step for [a] man, one giant leap for mankind." An estimated 1 billion viewers around the world shared that first step, watching a ghostly black-and-white television image beamed back to them across the cislunar void. During the next 10 hours, wherever the moon was visible from earth, human beings looked up at it and thought, There are men there. Immediately after that realization came an inevitable question. In the weeks and months that followed their safe return to earth, Armstrong, Aldrin, and Collins toured the world as international heroes, and everywhere they went, they were asked, "What was it like to go to the moon?"

In answering, the *Apollo 11* astronauts (or the 18 subsequent Apollo astronauts) would probably have started by describing the launch. Because of the *Saturn* V booster, the blast-off of the *Apollo/Saturn* rocket ship was an awe-inspiring and exhilarating experience for everybody involved. It was also arguably the single most dangerous part of the mission.

The *Saturn* V was the biggest, most powerful liquid-fueled rocket ever launched and flown successfully. Those

Assembly of the Apollo/Saturn *rocket ship was a job of titanic proportions. Here, inside the vehicle assembly building at the Kennedy Space Center, the command-service module and the lunar-module adaptor are about to be placed atop the third stage of the* Saturn *booster.*

seeing it for the first time often thought it was an impossible object, a monument to engineering hubris. It just seemed too *big* to fly. Well over 300 feet tall, it dwarfed its NASA predecessor boosters, the *Redstone*, *Atlas*, and *Titan*, as well as the Soviet A-Type and *Proton* (D-Type) boosters. The immense structure at Cape Canaveral (called the vehicle assembly building) that was used to house the *Saturn* during its construction could be described as the world's largest work shed; it covers 8 acres and has 525-foot-high walls and 456-foot-high (48-stories-high) doors. Soon after the vehicle assembly building was finished, rumors circulated that it was so big it had to be constantly air conditioned to keep clouds from forming inside.

The *Saturn* was a three-stage booster. Each stage was built by a different private contractor. The first stage (the lowermost stage in the stack), known as the S-IC, was put together at a Boeing plant in Louisiana. It was powered by 5 F-1 rocket engines, which, at lift-off, gulped an astonishing 3,333 gallons of kerosene and liquid oxygen per second, generating 7.6 million pounds' thrust (180 million horsepower).

The second, middle stage of the *Saturn* booster—the S-II—was built by North American Aviation at Seal

Once assembly of the Apollo/Saturn *was finished, the rocket ship and the service-umbilical tower were moved, intact, from the vehicle assembly building to the launchpad, which was more than three miles away. As seen here, this task was accomplished with the help of a Herculean vehicle known as the crawler.*

Beach, California. The S-II was powered by five J-2 engines, which burned liquid oxygen and liquid hydrogen as fuel. The S-II generated 1 million pounds' thrust.

The third, final stage—the S-IVB—came from Mc-Donnell Douglas in Sacramento, California. Its boosting duties were relatively light compared to the first two stages, so it used only a single J-2, generating the final 200,000 pounds' thrust needed for translunar injection.

Fully assembled and fueled—it took 10 hours to fill the fuel tanks—the *Apollo/Saturn* stack stood 363 feet tall and weighed more than 6 million pounds. On launch day, the sight of the rocket ship inspired feelings of awe not only in spectators but in many of the astronauts who were about to ride it. Mike Collins described it as "truly a monster." *Apollo 16* astronaut Ken Mattingly gave his impression of the *Apollo/Saturn* poised for launch: "There's frost on the sides of the cold cryogenic tanks [tanks that superchilled the oxygen and hydrogen to keep them in a liquid state] and there's little vapors coming out. When you look at it, it doesn't look like an inanimate hunk of machinery . . . You have this feeling that it's alive."

For Apollo astronauts on launch day, riding up the umbilical tower elevator was a tense and often bittersweet experience. For many of them, that was the time when the true implications of their situation hit home. "We were looking around a lot," *Apollo 15* astronaut James B. Irwin recalled. "We didn't want to miss anything because for all we knew, it might be our last time to see things on Earth." The astronauts thought of their families, their friends, their lives on earth, their place in history. And there was always, despite the supreme self-confidence shared by all astronauts and the confidence they had in NASA, the nagging doubt, as expressed in three simple words by Jim Irwin: "Will it work?"

While the astronauts were settling into the cockpit of the CM, the launch control center, located in the vehicle assembly building about 3 miles away from the pad, was buzzing with the activity of about 1,000 NASA launch technicians and engineers, almost all of them men in white shirts and neckties. Presiding over the scene was the launch director. (The original Apollo launch director was Rocco Petrone.) Gathered around the computer consoles and in front of the huge tracking screens in the firing room, the personnel at Cape Canaveral did for the first 10 minutes of the flight what mission control in Houston would do for the rest of it.

Lift-off was the single most spectacular occurrence of the entire mission. For many spectators it was a revelation of sorts. Most witnesses agree that the most impressive aspect of the launch is not the eruption of fire from beneath the rocket or the sight of the rocket rising slowly, literally inch by inch at first, from the caldron of smoke and flame, but rather the sound of the S-IC booster igniting. Aside from above-ground H-bomb tests, it is thought to be the loudest noise ever produced on earth. Mike Collins, who witnessed the launch of *Apollo 10* from about four miles away, wrote: "God, it's not a noise, it's a presence. . . . [It] reaches out and grabs you, and shakes, and as it crackles and roars, suddenly you realize the meaning of 7.5 million pounds of thrust."

About nine seconds before lift-off, the five F-1 engines begin firing. The rocket is secured to the launchpad by hold-down clamps, and it strains against them as the engines build up thrust. When sufficient thrust is achieved, the clamps release the rocket, which begins its ascent. These are excruciating seconds for the launch personnel in the firing room. Their worst fear is the pad fall-back scenario, in which the rocket loses power and falls back to the launchpad, initiating a holocaust.

For the astronauts, the first moments of lift-off defy description. "It feels just like it sounds" was all Jim Irwin could say. Usually the astronauts were rendered speechless during lift-off and ascent, although sometimes launch controllers would receive some indication of what they were experiencing, such as one astronaut's exhilarated "Yahoo!"

Two minutes, 40 seconds later, the F-I engines have consumed 559,218 gallons of liquid oxygen and kerosene and the *Apollo/Saturn* vehicle is 57 miles downrange. All the propellants in the 138-foot-long first stage are gone, so it is discarded and falls into the ocean. The second stage kicks in. Nine minutes, twelve seconds after lift-off, the second stage is spent and it too is discarded. If all has gone well, the rocket ship is now more than 1,000 miles from the Kennedy Space Center, and the third stage will finish the task of boosting the spacecraft into earth orbit. That is, if there have been no *anomalies*, NASA's word for problems of an unforeseen nature.

During the launch-and-ascent sequence of *Apollo 12*, NASA's second lunar expedition, the astronauts and ground control were presented with a major anomaly. The *Apollo 12* mission was an attempt at a precision lunar landing; the astronauts would try to land the LM in the Ocean of Storms, in the near vicinity of *Surveyor 3*, one of a series of probes sent to the moon by NASA in 1967. Charles "Pete" Conrad, Jr., commanded *Apollo 12*. Command module pilot was Richard F. Gordon, Jr. Conrad and Gordon had flown together on *Gemini 11*. Conrad had also flown aboard *Gemini 5*. Alan L. Bean was lunar module pilot; this was his first spaceflight. All three astronauts were navy veterans, so they named their CSM *Yankee Clipper* and their LM *Intrepid*. Launch day for *Apollo 12* was November 14, 1969.

It was a drizzly, overcast morning. A search plane reported no lightning within 24 miles of the pad, so NASA decided to proceed with the launch. Ignition, lift-off, and ascent went as planned until 36 seconds into the flight. As the *Apollo/Saturn* climbed into the low clouds, a bolt of lightning arced between the rocket and the ground. Twenty seconds later, a second bolt of lightning struck the

(continued on page 66)

A camera mounted atop the
umbilical tower 360 feet above
the ground provided this close-up
view of the launch of the Apollo/
Saturn rocket ship. Ignition has
just occurred and the five F-1
engines in the first stage are
building up thrust.

Lift-off occurs as the S-IC booster
stage achieves more than 7
million pounds' thrust and the
Apollo/Saturn breaks gravity's
hold and begins its ascent.

The Apollo/Saturn *climbs past the umbilical tower. The first stage of the booster was programmed to propel the rocket not only up but away from the tower as well—any contact between the rocket and the scaffolding following lift off would be disastrous.*

Riding a pillar of fire, the Apollo/Saturn *roars up and away.* "You're most anxious during the first fifteen seconds after lift-off," Apollo 17 astronaut Gene Cernan recalled. "If you lose one of those five engines in the first stage . . . you're going to come right back down on the pad."

(continued from page 63)

Twenty seconds later, a second bolt of lightning struck the rocket. Flight controllers heard a 20-second burst of static over their headsets and lost radio contact with the spacecraft. In the *Yankee Clipper* cockpit, Conrad saw a flash of light outside the front window and then "a glow inside the cabin." The control panel lit up "like a Christmas tree" as all the warning lights came on at once. About 20 seconds after that, the static faded and flight controllers heard Conrad again. He had some disturbing information to relay to mission control: "Okay, we just lost the platform, gang. I don't know what happened here. We had everything in the world drop out."

Conrad's words sent mission control into a scramble. What the astronaut meant by "We had everything in the world drop out" was that the lightning had opened all the circuit breakers in the CSM, knocking out its fuel cells and electrical system. Despite the thousands of hours of simulated disaster scenarios flight controllers endured to prepare for a flight, they had never trained for this anomaly, which launch director Rocco Petrone later christened "the Benjamin Franklin situation." Nevertheless, within three minutes, mission control had figured out how to correct the problem and passed the information on to the crew. *Yankee Clipper* was restored to normal power.

But as *Apollo 12* reached orbit there was still one major problem. The lightning had knocked out the inertial measurement unit—the "platform" that Conrad had reported to be "lost" to mission control—that was the heart of the *Yankee Clipper*'s guidance and navigation system. Unless the platform was realigned, the mission would have to be aborted. Mission control could not help the astronauts in this situation; they would have to realign the platform themselves by establishing their position relative to certain stars, an extremely difficult process. Using a sextant, the best friend of navigators since the days of the first ocean voyages, pilot Dick Gordon made the necessary star sightings out the spacecraft's window, entered the data into the

Yankee Clipper's computer, and thus managed to realign the guidance platform. Flight controllers decided that the spacecraft was fit to continue its mission, and the *Yankee Clipper* flew on to the moon.

The rest of the *Apollo 12* mission was an unqualified success. LM *Intrepid* landed on the Ocean of Storms on November 19, just 600 feet from *Surveyor 3*, a triumph for NASA's navigation specialists. Three hours after touchdown, Conrad and Bean began their first lunar traversal. *Apollo 12* carried the first Apollo lunar surface experiments package (ALSEP), an automated scientific laboratory that the astronauts would deploy and leave behind. The ALSEP monitored lunar seismic activity ("moon quakes"),

Apollo 12 *mission-commander Charles Conrad, Jr., holding a sample of lunar soil, and lunar-module pilot Alan L. Bean, whose reflection can be seen in Conrad's visor, engage in extravehicular activity following a successful lunar landing, November 19, 1969.*

the moon's magnetic field, and solar wind (charged particles, or plasma, radiated by the sun). After deploying the
ALSEP, the astronauts took a seven-hour rest inside the
LM, and then they began their second excursion, during
which they retrieved parts from *Surveyor 3* and collected
75 pounds of lunar samples.

Yankee Clipper's homeward journey was completed
without mishap, and the spacecraft splashed down in the
Pacific Ocean on November 24. The *Apollo 12* mission
made significant steps in the areas of precision lunar landings, lunar excursions—during their moon walks Conrad
and Bean covered six times the area covered by Armstrong

and Aldrin—and scientific research. But the most important aspect of *Apollo 12* was NASA's success in dealing
with an in-flight crisis. Mission control and the astronauts,
as well as all the other support systems, had performed
well in handling a situation that had been entirely un-
expected. In retrospect, the *Apollo 12* crisis can be viewed
as a fortuitous event, because it initiated NASA to the kind
of stress and pressure that would result from a serious, life-
threatening anomaly. Simulations helped in this area, but
there was no substitute for the real thing. And the next
mission, *Apollo 13*, would push NASA to the very limits
of its resourcefulness.

Apollo 12 *astronauts Conrad,
Bean, and Richard Gordon during
recovery operations in the Pacific
Ocean following the splashdown
of the* Yankee Clipper.

Lifeboat

Apollo 13 *insignia*

Implicit in the perennial "What was it like up there?" was another, darker, and less often voiced question— "What if something had gone wrong up there?" Fortunately, the astronauts on the first two lunar-landing missions did not encounter any problems that could not be solved, or that did not resolve themselves, fairly quickly. The *Apollo 13* astronauts, on the other hand, were confronted with NASA's worst nightmare—an accident that disabled the spacecraft to the point that the crew's safe return to earth was in jeopardy.

A superstitious person looking at the times and dates (not to mention the mission number) of *Apollo 13* would conclude that it was doomed from the start. *Apollo 13* was launched 13 minutes into the 13th hour of the day. Three days into the flight, on April 13, there was bad luck indeed, and NASA was faced with an anomaly of catastrophic proportions and potentially tragic consequences.

Apollo 13 lifted off on April 11, 1970. James A. Lovell, Jr., a seasoned 42-year-old astronaut who had flown on *Geminis* 7 and 12 and *Apollo 8*, was mission commander. John L. Swigert, Jr., was pilot for the CM *Odyssey*, and Fred W. Haise, Jr., was pilot for the LM *Aquarius*; both men were spaceflight rookies. They were bound for the mountainous Fra Mauro region of the moon (named after a medieval cartographer), where they hoped to continue investigations into the lunar geological makeup.

The Apollo 13 *rocket ship blasts off from launchpad complex 39A at the Kennedy Space Center, April 11, 1970. The destination of astronauts James A. Lovell, Jr., John L. Swigert, Jr., and Fred W. Haise was the moon's Fra Mauro highlands. But an oxygen-tank explosion in deep space put the mission—and the lives of the men—in jeopardy.*

At about nine o'clock on the night of April 13, as the spacecraft entered the final phase of the translunar passage, an explosion rocked the *Odyssey*. Alarms went off, warning lights flashed, and the CM vibrated with aftershocks. The astronauts were bewildered. "I really didn't know what happened, but I couldn't imagine why it was so loud," recalled Lovell. "I looked up at Fred Haise, and I knew Fred didn't know what the story was. Then I looked over at Jack Swigert, and Jack's eyes were as big as saucers." Swigert thought at first that the spacecraft had been "hit by a meteorite."

The astronauts began moving about the cabin to try to figure out what was going on. They soon learned that the explosion had damaged two of the CM's main fuel cells. (The fuel cells combined hydrogen and oxygen in a chemical reaction to generate electricity. The oxygen for the fuel cells, as well as the oxygen for the life-support system, was carried in the same cryogenic tanks.) This was a bitter discovery for the astronauts, for they knew that it eliminated any chance for them to complete the mission. But there was worse to come. Lovell, checking out the gauges for the *Odyssey*'s two oxygen tanks, was appalled to see that one of them read zero and the other was dropping steadily. Looking out the window, he saw "a gaseous substance venting at a very high rate of speed. It didn't take much intelligence for me to realize that the gas escaping from the back end of my spacecraft and the gauge on the second [oxygen] tank were one and the same, and that we would soon be completely out of oxygen in the command module." The astronauts were no longer concerned about missing out on a lunar landing—they were concerned about getting home alive.

It took longer for the true severity of the situation to register at mission control in Houston. At first, sitting in front of their computer screens, flight controllers and technicians simply could not believe the information they were receiving. They were getting indications of a massive loss of power and oxygen. Something they had thought was virtually impossible had occurred—two fuel cells as well as two oxygen tanks had failed. The odds against this happening were calculated to be something like 1 in 100 million. Nevertheless, it had happened. There was no time to search for the cause of the problem (months later, investigators would determine that the cause of the accident was an explosion in one of the oxygen tanks, which was in turn the result of a long sequence of minor engineering errors and miscommunications dating back to 1968, when

The original crew for the unlucky Apollo 13 was James Lovell, Jr., (left), Thomas K. Mattingly II (center), and Fred Haise. Mattingly came down with the measles shortly before launch day and was replaced by John Swigert.

the tank in question was accidentally dropped to the floor at a North American Aviation plant). Mission control now had to figure out how to get the astronauts home alive, and the pressure in the second oxygen tank was dropping by the second. The *Odyssey*, as one flight controller put it, was "dying."

Lovell, Swigert, and Haise were more than 200,000 miles away from home. Their trajectory had been altered by the explosion, but they were still headed away from earth and toward the moon, and their momentum was such that they were past the point where they could abort the flight without first orbiting the moon and using its gravity as a brake. Despite the efforts of mission control engineers and the astronauts themselves, the *Odyssey*'s power and life-support system could not be revived; within a matter of hours, the CM would have no light, no heat, no electricity, and no oxygen.

The idea of using the lunar module *Aquarius* as a "lifeboat" dawned on mission control and the astronauts at about the same time. It was the only remaining option. Mission control informed the astronauts, who had just come to the same conclusion, that they would have to shut down and evacuate the CM and climb into the LM, which had its own power supply and life-support system. Apparently undamaged by the explosion, the LM might function as a lifeboat for the astronauts to get home in.

While the beleaguered Lovell, Swigert, and Haise began moving from the dying CM into the LM, mission control was trying to answer a multitude of life-or-death questions. Would the LM, which had been designed to carry two men on a short, orbit-to-surface-to-orbit journey, have enough oxygen and electrical power to get them home? The spacecraft could not be simply turned around now; they were going to have to circumnavigate the moon and use its gravitational force and the LM descent engine to slingshot them back toward the earth; would there be enough fuel for this maneuver? And what about navigation? The essential data from the CM's guidance system would have to be transferred to the LM's guidance system if they hoped to find planet earth again. This chore required some tortuous mathematical computations, which a severely stressed Lovell was required to make by hand, with pencil and paper, in about 15 minutes time. A small mistake in these calculations could cause them to miss their little blue planet by hundreds of miles, in which case they they would, in Lovell's words, become "a perpetual monument to the space program," locked in a distant earth orbit that would continue long after they had run out of air to breathe. By the end of the first 24 hours of the crisis, NASA had mobilized every possible resource to get the astronauts home. Because they had never trained for—or even considered—many of the problems they now faced, the engineers, flight controllers, and designers were forced to improvise, and they proved to be creative and resourceful as well as tireless. In the meantime, news of the unfolding drama spread around the world, and the response was remarkable. The plight of the astronauts touched people everywhere, and offers of assistance poured into NASA and the White House. Even the Soviet Union, the United States's bitter rival, was ready to help. Premier Alexey N. Kosygin sent a message to President Richard Nixon informing him that "the Soviet Government has given orders to all citizens and members of the armed forces to use all necessary means to render assistance in the rescue of the American astronauts."

For the astronauts it was an ordeal. Once the crippled spacecraft had looped around the moon and was on an earthbound trajectory, the crew faced a three-day journey back across cislunar space. Drinking water was a by-product of the fuel cells. With the loss of the cells, careful rationing was necessary, and the astronauts became dehydrated. *Aquarius* had no system for heating water, so all their rehydrated meals were eaten cold. And with all

During their harrowing journey
back to earth, the Apollo 13 *crew*
was in danger of asphyxiation
when the filters that purged the
lunar module of carbon dioxide
were used up. In this photo,
Swigert is attempting to jerry-rig
a new air-scrubbing system.

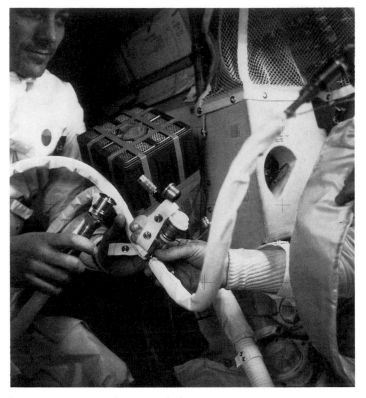

its systems operating at minimum power to conserve en-
ergy, the spacecraft became uncomfortably cold. Temperatures dropped to near freezing, and water condensed
on the walls and instrument panels, giving the craft a cold,
dank climate.

Various problems arose, some merely nagging, others
life threatening. The LM's life-support system was designed to sustain two persons for two days, not three astronauts for a three-day transearth crossing. Subsequently,
the chemical filters that removed carbon dioxide from the
cabin's atmosphere soon became depleted, and the astronauts were in danger of asphyxiation. There were plenty
of filters in the CM, but they did not fit the LM system.
So, using cardboard from the covers of their flight-rules
manuals, plastic storage bags, and adhesive tape, the astronauts modified the CM filters to fit the LM. Another

The square package attached to a hose is the improvised carbon-dioxide scrubber constructed by the resourceful Apollo 13 *astronauts out of adhesive tape, pieces of cardboard, and lithium filters from the defunct command-module* Odyssey.

problem concerned the spacecraft's trajectory. The LM had not been built to act as the CM's tugboat, and it kept drifting out of the proper trajectory and attitude (its position relative to a fixed point such as the earth or a star). Mission control came up with an especially imaginative procedure for Lovell to use to realign the spacecraft. The procedure involved using the earth's terminator (the line dividing the light and dark portions of the earth as seen from space) as a reference point, and it worked.

In this manner, like men in a leaky lifeboat using whatever was at hand to plug the holes, Lovell, Swigert, and Haise, with the help of mission control, coaxed and prodded their spacecraft toward the earth. The final and most hazardous phase for *Apollo 13* would be the spacecraft's reentry into the earth's atmosphere. Virtually every aspect of reentry, which was always a risky proposition, would be subject to new—and potentially deadly—variables. The astronauts would have to return to earth in the *Odyssey*, using the CM's reentry power supply—if they could get it started by using the LM's batteries. Had the heat shield been damaged in the explosion? If it had been, the spacecraft would be incinerated when it hit the earth's atmosphere. The LM also would have to be jettisoned before they hit the atmosphere, another touch-and-go maneuver.

Lovell, waking from a restless three-hour sleep on April 17, considered the reentry situation they were about to confront. Physically and mentally drained, hungry, thirsty, and unshaven, in a freezing, cramped, and damaged spacecraft hurtling toward the earth at thousands of miles per hour, the mission commander weighed their chances for survival. Lovell's subsequent comment to his two companions was a classic example of astronaut understatement. "It's going to be interesting today," he said.

The drama of *Apollo 13* ended shortly after noon on April 17 with two tired words—"Okay, Joe." That was Jack Swigert's exhausted reply to the flight controller who was

No splashdown celebration in mission control was as heartfelt as the one that took place following the safe return of the Apollo 13 astronauts. From left to right, the first three men in front are NASA flight directors Gerald D. Griffin, Eugene F. Kranz, and Glynn S. Lunney. In the upper left corner, Manned Spacecraft Center deputy director Christopher C. Kraft lights the celebratory cigar of director Robert R. Gilruth.

hailing the *Odyssey* over the radio. All contact with the astronauts had been lost about six minutes before because of the ionization that occurred when the spacecraft plunged into the earth's atmosphere. To the NASA personnel at mission control, the sound of Swigert's voice meant that reentry had been successful. About four minutes later, television screens around the world showed the *Odyssey*, swinging gently under its orange and white parachutes, break through the clouds and float gently down to the ocean.

Tired, undernourished, and unshaven, the Apollo 13 *astronauts are given a rousing reception aboard the* Iwo Jima *shortly after their recovery from the splashdown site in the Pacific. Haise (left), Swigert (center), and Lovell wear the smiles of men who are glad to be home.*

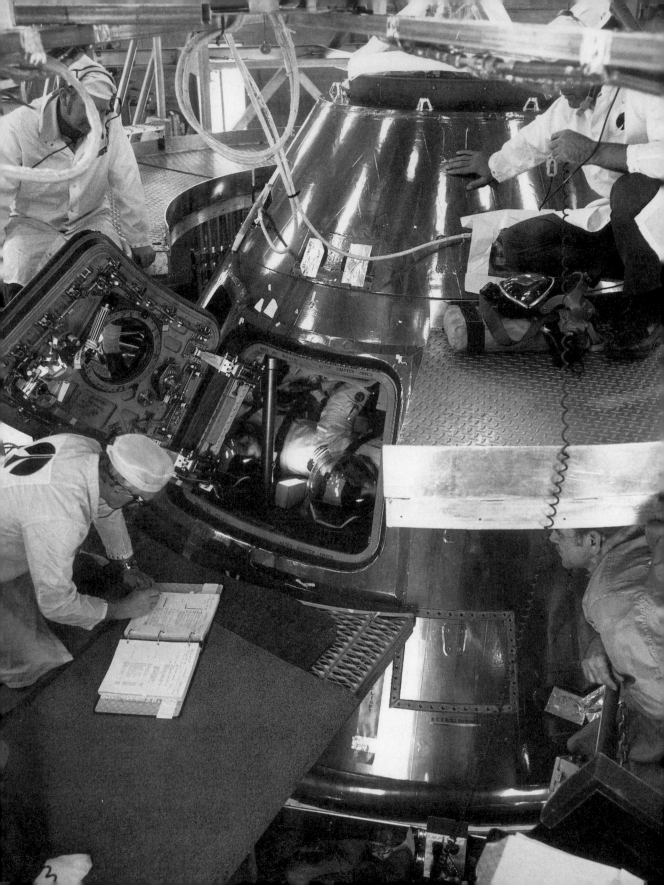

Mountains of the Moon

Apollo 14 *insignia*

Apollo 13 was a severe test for NASA. It was also, in many ways, NASA's finest hour. Although the mission was technically a "failure," the only manned Apollo flight that had to be aborted, the performance of the astronauts and the support personnel on earth was exceptional, and NASA proved that it was able to handle a crisis of major proportions. Nevertheless, as with the *Apollo 1* disaster (and the space-shuttle *Challenger* tragedy in 1986), the subsequent launch schedule was delayed as an investigation into the cause of the accident was mounted, and the next mission did not lift off until January 1971.

Because of the *Apollo 13* misadventure, *Apollo 14* took on a vital importance for NASA, much like the flights that immediately followed the deaths of Grissom, Chaffee, and White. Despite the heroic behavior of just about everyone involved in the drama, public support for the program was declining rapidly, and consequently, congressional support was weakening as well. NASA hoped to launch seven more flights after *Apollo 13*. They knew that if there was a problem with mission *14*, the entire program would most likely be aborted for lack of its most essential fuel— not liquid oxygen or hydrogen, but money granted by Congress. (So far, each manned lunar-landing had cost about $400 million.) For NASA, *Apollo 14* was yet another do-or-die situation.

NASA *technicians check out the command-module* Endeavour *prior to its July 1971 launch. After* Apollo 14, *the objectives of NASA's manned lunar missions changed. Scientific discovery, rather than pure exploration, became the focus of Project Apollo, and corresponding modifications were introduced into the equipment.*

If *Apollo 14* mission commander Alan Shepard felt any of the pressure associated with the mission, he did not show it. The 47-year-old Shepard, as everyone knew, was on intimate terms with the stress generated by the uncertainties of a NASA manned mission. He had been the first American in outer space, having piloted NASA's first manned spacecraft, the Mercury program's *Freedom 7*, on May 3, 1961. A navy captain from New Hampshire, Shepard was known as the Ice Commander for his perennial cool under pressure. Shepard was also familiar with the stress generated by what was probably an astronaut's second-worst fear (death by fire being the first)—being grounded. Afflicted with Ménière's disease, an inner ear condition, Shepard had been forced into an administrative role during Gemini and Apollo. Despite such galling bad luck, the crusty Shepard had never given up his dream of returning to outer space, and in 1968 an experimental operation improved his condition enough for his flight status to be upgraded, and he was reinserted into the mission rotation as commander for *Apollo 14*.

The LM pilot for *Apollo 14* was 41-year-old navy veteran Edgar D. Mitchell. CM pilot for the mission was 36-year-old air force fighter pilot Stuart A. Roosa. Although neither man had flown in outer space before—the boyish Roosa seemed especially green compared to the grizzled first American in space—it would not take them long to shed their rookie status. The *Apollo 14* command module was called *Kitty Hawk*; the lunar module was named *Antares*. Mitchell and Shepard would attempt to set the *Antares* down in the moon's rugged Fra Mauro highlands, at best a treacherous landing site.

Apollo 14 lifted off on January 31, 1971. Because of the previous mission, everyone in NASA was hoping for a smooth, uneventful flight. But those who had been with the space program for a long time knew that there was no such thing as an uneventful spaceflight, and it did not take long for the first serious problem to manifest itself.

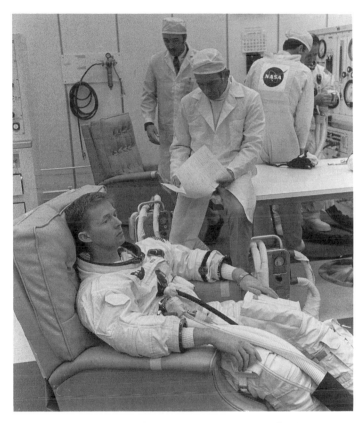

Director of flight-crew operations Donald K. ("Deke") Slayton examines a prelaunch checklist as Apollo 14 *command-module pilot Stuart A. Roosa undergoes final pressure-suit tests.* Apollo 14 *was launched on January 31, 1971.*

After a successful translunar injection, CM pilot Stu Roosa began the transposition and docking procedure. Roosa separated the CM *Kitty Hawk* from the *Saturn*'s third stage and the LM *Antares*, moved the mother ship a short distance away, turned around and attempted to dock with the LM adaptor. But the CM's drogue would not lock in the adaptor. Roosa backed off and tried again, and again. Still the adaptor refused to accept the CM. For two hours, Roosa courted the LM in this manner while anxiety levels rose to new heights in mission control. Finally, Roosa slammed the drogue into the adaptor with considerable force, and the impact triggered the capture latches. The problem was solved for the time being, but the astronauts and mission control could not help wondering what would happen during the lunar-orbit-rendezvous docking.

The cislunar transit, to the relief of everybody, was completed without incident. On the fifth day of the mission, while the spacecraft orbited the moon, Shepard and Mitchell entered the *Antares* and undocked. As the LM established itself in orbit and the two astronauts prepared for descent to the lunar surface, the abort light on the LM's instrument panel began to flash. Shepard and Mitchell were appalled. Mission control quickly learned that the flashing light was a false alarm caused by a malfunction in the LM's computer guidance system. Nevertheless, the alarm could trigger the LM's automatic abort sequence, which would prevent the *Antares* from making a lunar landing.

To come so close to the moon's surface only to be stopped short was unacceptable. (Mitchell asserted later that it was something "we just couldn't live with.") Once again, NASA scrambled to find a solution to a computer conundrum while the frustrated astronauts sweated in lunar orbit. With the help of specialists from the Massachusetts Institute of Technology in Cambridge, where the LM's guidance system had been designed, and technicians from Grumman Engineering Corporation in New York, where the LM was built, NASA devised a way to reprogram the *Antares* computer to override the abort signal. Mitchell, in a prodigious display of key punching, managed to accomplish this task in 10 minutes, and Shepard coolly guided the *Antares* through the jagged ridges of the Fra Mauro region to a safe landing in the midst of the Doublet and Triplet crater clusters. "It's a beautiful day in the land of Fra Mauro," Shepard declared.

While Stu Roosa circled the moon in the *Kitty Hawk* and carried out a photomapping assignment, Shepard and Mitchell completed two four-and-a-half-hour moon walks, in the process covering more lunar territory than all of the previous Apollo astronauts combined. Their second excursion was an arduous trek across the Fra Mauro wastes in an attempt to find Cone Crater, a 250-foot-deep chasm that they believed was located somewhere in the vicinity of their landing site. Although they never located the crater—"Gee whiz, we can't stop without looking into the Cone Crater," Mitchell lamented when mission control advised them to turn back—their surface exploration was fruitful. With the help of a wagonlike contraption called the modularized equipment transporter, the astronauts deployed another ALSEP and collected more than 95 pounds of moon rocks. Perhaps the most memorable part of the *Apollo 14* mission occurred at the end of the astronauts' second moon walk, when Shepard produced a makeshift golf club and three golf balls he had smuggled to the moon. A television camera had been set up outside the *Antares*, and perplexed earth audiences were treated to the bizarre sight of the astronaut driving golf balls for 500 yards over the desolate lunar landscape.

Apollo 15 *insignia*

Despite fears that the *Antares* might have problems docking with the mother ship following the lunar orbit rendezvous, Shepard and Mitchell rejoined Roosa without any mishaps, and the astronauts splashed safely down in the Pacific on February 9, 1971. NASA had proved that it could still put men on the moon and "return [them] safely to earth," as JFK had proposed. Nevertheless, political and public support for the Apollo program was at a new low. Many Americans believed that their government could no longer afford Apollo's gigantic price tag, especially when the money might be used to heal some of the country's more terrestrial—and immediate—domestic ills. For these citizens, lunar exploration seemed frivolous. And, incredibly, a lot of Americans had simply become bored with the ongoing moon program. The multitudes who had watched *Apollo 11* on television were not tuning in anymore. Once men had been on the moon, further landings seemed gratuitous.

It was partly for these reasons (and partly because NASA had planned from the beginning to change the program's emphasis for the final series of missions) that *Apollo 15* represented a change in NASA's lunar program. *Apollos 11, 12, 13,* and *14* can be classified as pure exploration. It might be said that NASA first went to the moon for the same reason mountaineer Sir Edmund Hillary first climbed Mount Everest—"Because it was there." The final three lunar missions, however, would be exercises in scientific exploration. Through *Apollos 15, 16,* and *17,*

NASA hoped to ensure a future for itself by proving how important and valuable lunar exploration was for the enrichment of humankind's knowledge of the universe. "Ours was labeled the first extended scientific mission to the moon," observed *Apollo 15* LM pilot Jim Irwin, "and that's exactly what it was. It was science." *Apollo 15*'s LM *Falcon*, carrying mission commander David R. Scott and

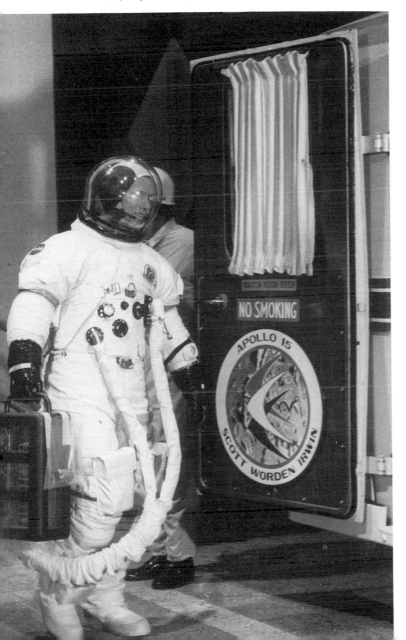

Sealed inside their pressure suits and carrying portable oxygen units, Apollo 15 mission commander David Scott, command-module pilot Alfred M. Worden, and lunar-module pilot James Irwin walk past well-wishers to the van that will transport them to the launchpad, July 26, 1971.

LM pilot Irwin, landed in the mountainous Hadley-Apennine region on July 30, 1971. CM pilot Alfred M. Worden orbited overhead in the mother ship *Endeavour*. Both the command module and the lunar module were equipped with new scientific paraphernalia. The *Endeavour*'s service module now contained a scientific instrument bay, which housed an array of instruments that would allow Worden to study the moon in more detail than any CM pilot before him. These instruments included three different spectrometers that could help scientists determine the composition of the moon's surface; two high-resolution cameras; and a laser altimeter that provided precise altitude data. Also

A NASA dietary technician packages dehydrated space food to be eaten on the moon by Apollo 15's David R. Scott and James B. Irwin, who would spend more time on the lunar surface than any previous astronauts.

carried in the scientific instrument bay was a 78.5 pound subsatellite that, once deployed, would gather data on lunar gravitational and electrical fields.

Meanwhile, down on the surface, Scott and Irwin climbed out of the *Falcon* to begin the first of three scheduled excursions. Like Worden, they had new equipment to try out. The most important new device the earthlings had brought to the moon was the lunar roving vehicle, or moon rover. The moon rover was a white topless, battery-powered buggy weighing 460 pounds. Designed and built

The Apollo 15 mission featured a new piece of equipment—the lunar roving vehicle, which would allow the astronauts to drive around on the moon and explore more territory than ever before. In this photo, NASA engineers are fitting the folded lunar rover to the LM Falcon, which will carry the four-wheeled vehicle to the moon.

by Boeing and General Motors at a cost of about $12 million, the rover would carry the two space-suited astronauts, 120 pounds of scientific equipment, 100 pounds of communications equipment, and 60 pounds of lunar samples. Each of the rover's four wheels contained a one-quarter-horsepower electric motor, allowing a top speed

of about eight miles per hour. NASA hoped that the rover would give the astronauts the mobility to venture far away from the landing site.

Scott and Irwin unfolded the rover from its storage place on the side of the *Falcon* and then set up the portable television camera that would carry color images of the

Leaving the parked moon rover, astronaut David Scott takes a stroll and examines a lunar boulder. Investigating the geological makeup of the moon was the prime objective of the final three Apollo missions.

moon back to earth audiences, allowing them to accompany the two astronauts on their lunar drives. The area NASA wanted the astronauts to explore was the Hadley-Apennine region, a Rocky Mountain–like range that lay between the Sea of Rains (Mare Imbrium) and the Sea of Serenity (Mare Serenitatis). Their first ride in the rover was a brief jaunt to the edge of Hadley Rille, a gaping chasm that could easily swallow the vehicle and its occupants if an accident occurred. Upon return to the landing site, they set up their ALSEP, a laser reflector (bouncing a laser beam from earth off the reflector, scientists could determine the exact distance between the earth and the moon at a given time), and a solar-wind sampler. After six and a half hours on the surface they retired to the LM for some food and rest.

During the next two days, Scott and Irwin completed two more marathon excursions. For scientists on earth, it was a bonanza. The final two forays lasted more than 12 hours, during which the moon rover covered more than 14 miles of territory around the base of the craggy, desolate Apennine Mountains. The astronauts, using a specially designed, battery-powered drill, collected 170 pounds of rock and soil samples, including one rock that was of particular interest to scientists back on earth—a 4.5-billion-year-old chunk of the primordial lunar crust. The Genesis rock, as it was immediately dubbed, along with the other samples, photographs, and visual observations made by the astronauts, provided scientists with unprecedented clues to not only the geological makeup, age, and origin of the moon but to the origins of the entire solar system as well.

Like Alan Shepard, Mission Commander Scott performed a stunt for the television camera before he climbed into the LM for departure. Scott's demonstration was a little more serious than Shepard's round of lunar golf, and it seemed to underscore the new, purely scientific phase

Project Apollo had begun. Scott wanted to use the moon's lack of an atmosphere to demonstrate one of Galileo Galilei's most famous assertions. (Galileo Galilei was a Renaissance physicist, inventor, and astronomer of revolutionary impact who postulated that two objects falling in a vacuum will fall at the same rate no matter how heavy they are.) Holding up a feather and a hammer, Scott dropped them at the same time. Sure enough, they fell at the same rate and landed on the surface of the moon together. "How about that?" Scott said. Galileo, the first man to clearly see the surface of the moon through a telescope, would have approved.

In the Manned Spacecraft Center's lunar receiving laboratory, David Scott has a look at the so-called Genesis rock, which he discovered on the moon during an Apollo 15 lunar-surface excursion. The rock, thought to be more than 4 billion years old, contains clues to the origin of the solar system.

Being There

Apollo 16 *insignia*

What was it like on the moon? What did it look like? What did walking across its rough surface feel like to an earthling? The astronauts of NASA's final two lunar missions, *Apollo 16* and *Apollo 17*, were best qualified to answer these questions, for they spent the most time on the moon; so much time, in fact, that some of them professed that by the end of their visit they had actually begun to feel "at home" on that alien world.

Apollo 16 astronauts John W. Young and Charles M. Duke, Jr., set down the LM *Orion* on the boulder-strewn plains of the moon's Descartes region on April 20, 1972. (T. Kenneth Mattingly piloted the CM *Casper*.) Young and Duke, in carrying out the most extensive lunar science and reconnaissance program yet attempted by NASA, which included the first astronomical observations made by humans from a celestial body other than the earth, spent more than 20 hours outside the LM. And on December 11, 1972, the LM *Challenger* landed in the moon's Taurus-Littrow region. *Apollo 17* astronauts Eugene A. Cernan and Harrison H. Schmitt (the CM *America* was manned by Ronald E. Evans) spent even more time exploring, taking photographs, and collecting samples than the *Apollo 16* astronauts had.

Because the moon has no atmosphere, the astronauts who ventured outside the lunar module had to bring their own atmosphere with them inside their bulky pressure suit

Geologist Harrison H. Schmitt, NASA's first astronaut-scientist, uses a rakelike device called the Apollo lunar geology hand tool to collect rock samples from the moon's Taurus-Littrow region during the Apollo 17 mission. "I consider myself a flying geologist," Schmitt told the New York Times.

and helmet. The astronauts had a love/hate relationship
with their pressure suits, or moon cocoons; they were both
an awkward encumbrance and a life-supporting, oxygen-
giving womb. An astronaut fully suited for a moon walk
would be wearing what was known as an extravehicular

mobility unit (EMU), including gloves, boots, and helmet.
The EMU consisted of three layers: a liquid cooling garment to regulate the astronaut's body temperature; a pressure garment to contain the suit's artificial atmosphere;
and a thermal garment designed to repel micrometeoroids

Apollo 15 astronaut Jim Irwin,
the lunar module, and the lunar
rover, in a photograph taken by
David Scott during their 66-
hour-long stay on the moon. The
Apollo 16 astronauts spent even
more time on the lunar surface,
and by the time Apollo 17 was
completed, the idea of men
walking on the moon had lost
much of its novelty and excitement
for the American public.

Apollo 17 *insignia*

(tiny high-velocity particles) and protect the astronauts from the extreme temperatures of the lunar surface, which range from 250 degrees Farenheit in the sunlight to −250 degrees Farenheit in the shade. The micrometeoroid garment was reinforced with seven layers of Beta cloth, a synthetic fiber developed by ILC Industries of Delaware, which was in turn coated with Teflon. Each pressure suit cost about $100,000.

On the astronaut's back was a huge backpack known as the portable life-support system (PLSS), which carried the primary oxygen supply, the oxygen purge system, a backup oxygen supply, a water-cooling loop, and the voice communication systems. On the chest of the EMU was a remote control unit that contained a water pump, an oxygen fan, a communications selector switch and volume control, a camera mount, and sometimes a camera. The entire outfit, including a helmet with a gold-tinted visor to protect the astronaut's eyes from ultraviolet sunlight, weighed 180 pounds on earth, making it impossible to move around in. Under the moon's one-sixth gravity, however, it weighed only 30 pounds.

Before they could begin to actively observe their new environment, the astronauts had to adjust to life in this lesser gravity. Although all the astronauts who would land on the moon had been trained extensively with equipment that approximated the moon's one-sixth gravity, actually walking on the moon was always an entirely new experience. Stepping out of the LM, the astronauts would be pleasantly surprised at the new buoyancy afforded by its lesser gravity, and they all adopted a kind of skipping or hopping motion to move about. Once they were comfortable in their movements, they began to look around and fully experience their surroundings.

All the astronauts agreed that it was a desertlike landscape, a place of "stark beauty" and "magnificent desolation." The reported color of the powdery topsoil that covered the lunar surface, on the other hand, seemed to change with the perspective of each individual astronaut. Some claimed that it was entirely monochromatic or colorless. Gray, brown, tan, and black were frequently mentioned. Some found it to be "ashen" and "chalky" in appearance. Others encountered orange, rosy, or rust-colored topsoil. (According to Buzz Aldrin, who could smell it on his boots when he returned to the LM, the topsoil had a pungent scent, "like gunpowder or spent cap pistols.") At first glance, the color of the rocks strewn about the surface of the moon matched the color of the local topsoil, but closer examination revealed them to be made up of crystals of "all conceivable colors."

Each of the astronauts found the moon to be an eerie place, otherworldly in the truest sense of the word. Because the moon has no atmosphere, the astronauts found that its "skies" were as black as outer space, and the sunshine was pure and harsh, casting sharp shadows. And because it is so much smaller than the earth, the moon's horizon, as Buzz Aldrin noticed, "in all directions visibly curved down away from us." Those astronauts who landed in mountainous regions compared them to the mountains of the southwestern United States. In these areas the astronauts reported deep, stratified canyons and fantastic lava fields that were the result of centuries of episodic volcanic activity. None of the astronauts saw any signs of life.

Despite these alien wonders, the astronauts who explored the moon agreed that their most vivid memory was the sight of the earth from the surface of the moon. "It was the most fantastically beautiful thing I had ever seen," Charles Duke reported. "It looked like a Christmas tree ornament just hanging up there in the blackness, the jewel of Earth hung up in black velvet space."

Once they were back on earth, the lunar astronauts seemed to have trouble communicating to others the profound nature of their experience. *Apollo 17*'s Harrison Schmitt, one of the last two humans to walk on the moon, observed that "being there is the critical ingredient. That's

what distinguishes a meaningful experience from one
you've seen on television or in the movies or heard someone else talk about. I had tried to anticipate what it would
be like [to walk on the moon] for many years and particularly for the last fourteen months of training. But it was
obvious that there was no way that one could have antic-
ipated what it would be like to stand in the valley of Taurus-

Earthrise. According to Webster's Ninth New Collegiate Dictionary, *this word was coined in 1968 and is defined as "the rising of the earth above the horizon of the moon as seen from the moon."*

Littrow, or in any spot on the moon, and see this brilliantly illuminated landscape with a brighter sun than anyone had ever stood in before, with a blacker than black sky, and the mountains rising on either side to over 6,500 feet. And then to top this whole thing off in this blacker than black sky was a beautiful, brilliantly illuminated blue marble that we call Earth."

A number of the astronauts who walked on the moon experienced a similar—and remarkable—feeling upon leaving it. Once they had finished the business of lift-off from the lunar surface in the LM ascent stage—a particularly hair-raising event because there was no backup engine on the LM ascent stage, which left the astronauts with only one chance to get back to the mother ship— and had finished the LOR and the transearth injection as well, all of the astronauts felt a twinge of melancholy.

1. The Apollo 16 *lunar module* Orion *poised for lift-off from the moon. During this sequence, the landing gear and the bottom section of the LM (the descent stage) would serve as a launchpad for the upper compartment (the ascent stage), which would carry the astronauts back to the mother ship.*

2. The Orion's *ascent engine ignites, blowing away the metallic insulation covering the outside of the lunar module.*

3. The Orion *ascent stage achieves lift-off and begins to pull up and away from the descent stage. The LM ascent stage will now return to lunar orbit and an eventual rendezvous and docking with the mother ship.*

Watching the moon grow smaller as he left it behind, *Apollo 15*'s Jim Irwin realized that "camped in the shadow of the Apennine Mountains" he had "felt very comfortable, very protected. I felt quite at home and . . . I would have liked to have stayed there a longer time."

The *Apollo 17* CM *America* splashed down on December 19, 1972. The return to earth of astronauts Cernan, Evans, and Schmitt marked the end of Project Apollo. Although NASA had planned additional manned lunar

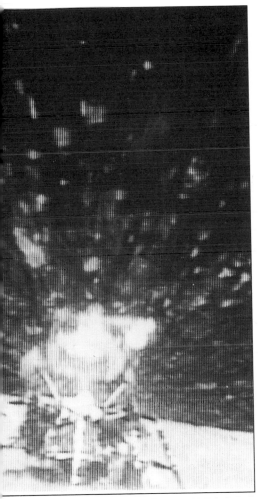

Each individual Apollo mission and Program Apollo itself ended with the welcome sight of a command module, parachutes deployed, drifting down to the waters of the Pacific Ocean.

landings, the program finally succumbed to a growing popular and political resentment. Things on earth were just too messed up, people seemed to think, to be spending billions of dollars on putting a man in a funny suit on the moon for two or three days. Many Americans had lost interest after *Apollo 11;* once you saw one lunar mission you had seen them all, TV viewers felt. The post-Apollo years saw a general decline in the public's interest in space exploration. Project Apollo became a fading memory, part of a time that had passed into the history books along with Richard Nixon, the Vietnam War, and Kent State.

The true historical significance of Project Apollo remains open to debate. Was it, as Neil Armstrong stated, a "giant leap for mankind?" Or was it merely a propaganda stunt, a prideful and wasteful expenditure of money and technological know-how? The argument has taken on a new importance as the millennium draws closer, bringing with it the distinct possibility of further manned exploration of the solar system and of the planet Mars in particular. Proponents of the Apollo program assert that it was perhaps the greatest event of the 20th century, humankind's inevitable first step outside the confines of the earth's atmosphere. Next stop—Mars! Detractors wonder if human beings are fit to explore the solar system when they are unable to keep their earthly affairs in order, and they point to the 90 tons of junk Project Apollo left behind on the surface of the moon as evidence of humankind's habit of polluting whatever environment they find themselves in.

Both arguments have merit, but it is the argument itself that is the most valuable legacy of Project Apollo. Humankind's greatest outward venture has resulted in some revealing and provocative inward exploration. Are we fit, as a species, to expand into the solar system? How have we treated our own planet, and subsequently, how will we treat other planets?

As they stood on the surface of the moon, the astronauts' gaze was not drawn outward into the blackness, toward the farther reaches of space; rather, it was drawn inevitably back toward the good earth. According to LM pilot Jim Irwin, the Apollo astronauts were given "a new appreciation for the earth. We've seen it from afar, we've seen it from the distance of the moon. We realize that the earth is the only natural home for man that we know of, and that we had better protect it."

Further Reading

Aldrin, Buzz, and Malcolm McConnell. *Men from Earth*. New York: Bantam Books, 1989.

Armstrong, Neil, et al. *First on the Moon*. Boston: Little, Brown, 1970.

Borman, Frank, with Robert J. Serling. *Countdown: An Autobiography*. New York: Morrow, 1988.

Brooks, Courtney G., James M. Grimwood, and Lloyd S. Swenson. *Chariots for Apollo: A History of Manned Lunar Spacecraft*. Washington, DC: Government Printing Office, 1979.

Clark, Philip. *The Soviet Manned Space Program*. New York: Crown, 1988.

Collins, Michael. *Carrying the Fire*. New York: Farrar, Straus & Giroux, 1974.

———. *Liftoff: The Story of America's Adventure in Space*. New York: Grove Press, 1988.

Compton, William David. *Where No Man Has Gone Before: A History of Apollo Lunar Exploration Missions*. Washington, DC: Government Printing Office, 1989.

Cooper, Henry S. *A House in Space*. New York: Holt, Rinehart & Winston, 1976.

Crouch, Tom D. *The National Aeronautics and Space Administration*. New York: Chelsea House, 1990.

Cunningham, Walter. *The All-American Boys*. New York: Macmillan, 1977.

Gatland, Kenneth. *Manned Spacecraft*. New York: Macmillan, 1976.

Hallion, Richard P., and Tom D. Crouch, eds. *Apollo: Ten Years Since Tranquility Base*. Washington, DC: Smithsonian Institution Press, 1979.

Hurt, Harry, III. *For All Mankind*. New York: Atlantic Monthly Press, 1988.

Kennedy, Gregory P. *The First Men in Space*. New York: Chelsea House, 1991.

McDougall, Walter A. *Heavens and the Earth: A Political History of the Space Age*. New York: Basic Books, 1985.

Murray, Charles, and Catherine Bly Cox. *Apollo: The Race to the Moon*. New York: Simon & Schuster, 1989.

National Aeronautics and Space Administration. *The First Twenty-five Years: 1958–1983*. Washington, DC: Government Printing Office, 1983.

Newkirk, Dennis. *Almanac of Soviet Manned Space Flight*. Houston: Gulf, 1990.

Schirra, Walter M., with Richard N. Billings. *Schirra's Space*. Boston: Quinlan Press, 1988.

Wolfe, Tom. *The Right Stuff*. New York: Farrar, Straus & Giroux, 1979.

Chronology

Entries in roman type refer directly to the Apollo mission to the moon and manned spaceflight; entries in italics refer to important historical and cultural events of the era.

March 1926	*American Robert H. Goddard launches the world's first liquid-propelled rocket in his aunt's Massachusetts cabbage patch; it achieves an altitude of 41 feet*
Oct. 1957	*The Soviet Union launches* Sputnik 1, *the world's first man-made earth satellite*
July 1958	The U.S. Congress passes the National Aeronautics and Space Act, thus creating the National Aeronautics and Space Administration (NASA); NASA begins project Mercury, the first American manned-spaceflight program
1961	In April, Yury Gagarin of the Soviet Union becomes the first human to orbit the earth; Alan Shepard becomes the first American in space one month later; President John F. Kennedy, in a speech to a joint session of Congress, urges a manned mission to the moon before the end of the decade
1963	*John F. Kennedy assassinated; Lyndon B. Johnson becomes president*
March 1966	*Gemini* 8 completes the first docking maneuver in space, an important step for a lunar landing
Jan. 1967	Astronauts Gus Grissom, Ed White, and Roger Chaffee die in a fire aboard *Apollo 1*

1968   *Apollo* 7 resumes manned spaceflight; first American circumlunar flight completed by *Apollo* 8 manned by astronauts William Anders, Frank Borman, and James Lovell; the mission deflates all Soviet hopes of putting a man on the moon first; *Richard Nixon elected president of the United States*

1969   *Apollo* missions 9 and 10 complete tests and are final dress rehearsals for the *Apollo 11* lunar-landing mission; astronauts Neil Armstrong, Buzz Aldrin, and Mike Collins are chosen for *Apollo 11*; lunar module *Eagle* touches down on the moon's surface; Neil Armstrong becomes the first human to walk on the moon; *Apollo* 12, manned by astronauts Charles "Pete" Conrad, Richard Gordon, and Alan Bean, successfully completes the second lunar landing; Conrad and Gordon land the lunar module *Intrepid* in the moon's Ocean of Storms

April 1970   Command module *Odyssey* becomes disabled in space; astronauts James Lovell, John Swigert, and Fred Haise use all of their resources to pilot the lunar module *Aquarius* safely back to earth

1971   *Apollo* 14, commanded by Alan Shepard, completes a lunar landing in the mountainous Fra Mauro region of the moon; *Apollo* 15 astronauts David Scott and James Irwin conduct the most extensive study yet of the lunar surface, collecting soil and rock samples through the use of the moon rover

1972   Because of excessive cost and public apathy, missions 16 and 17 wind up the *Apollo* program; astronauts Eugene Cernan and Harrison Schmitt become the last two humans to have walked on the moon

Index

Picture Credits

Gregory Kennedy is the director of the National Space Center at Alamagordo, New Mexico. A graduate of the University of Maryland, he has written several books on the subject of spaceflight, including *Rockets, Missiles, and Spacecraft of the National Air and Space Museum* as well as *The First Men in Space* in this series.

William H. Goetzmann holds the Jack S. Blanton, Sr., Chair in History at the University of Texas at Austin, where he has taught for many years. The author of numerous works on American history and exploration, he won the 1967 Pulitzer and Parkman prizes for his *Exploration and Empire: The Role of the Explorer and Scientist in the Winning of the American West, 1800–1900.* With his son William N. Goetzmann, he coauthored *The West of the Imagination,* which received the Carr P. Collins Award in 1986 from the Texas Institute of Letters. His documentary television series of the same name received a blue ribbon in the history category at the American Film and Video Festival held in New York City in 1987. A recent work, *New Lands, New Men: America and the Second Great Age of Discovery,* was published in 1986 to much critical acclaim.

Michael Collins served as command module pilot on the *Apollo 11* space mission, which landed his colleagues Neil Armstrong and Buzz Aldrin on the moon. A graduate of the United States Military Academy, Collins was named an astronaut in 1963. In 1966 he piloted the *Gemini 10* mission, during which he became the third American to walk in space. The author of several books on space exploration, Collins was director of the Smithsonian Institution's National Air and Space Museum from 1971 to 1978 and is a recipient of the Presidential Medal of Freedom.

28 DAYS

DATE DUE			